Francesca Walsh, Ian Jones and Nathan

# ESSENTIALS

## AQA GCSE
## Science A

# Contents

# Contents

*N.B. The numbers in brackets correspond to the reference numbers on the AQA Science A specification.*

1. List A contains some lifestyle choices. List B contains some health risks. **(3 marks)**

   Draw a line from each choice in List A to the associated health risk in List B.

   | **List A** | **List B** |
   |---|---|

   | List A | List B |
   |---|---|
   | Eating a diet high in animal fats | Heart attack |
   | Eating too much salt | Liver disease |
   | Eating too many high energy foods | High blood pressure |
   | Drinking excessive alcohol | Obesity |

2. Ron is overweight and wants to lose some weight. Suggest **two** things Ron could do to lose weight. **(2 marks)**

3. The following sentences are about cholesterol. Underline the correct words. **(3 marks)**

   Cholesterol is made in the **pancreas / liver**.

   **Inherited factors / weight** can affect how much cholesterol the body makes.

   Eating **saturated / unsaturated** fats increases blood cholesterol.

4. Elena has an ear infection. She goes to the doctor. The doctor says she has a bacterial infection.

   **(a)** What treatment might the doctor suggest to kill the bacteria? **(1 mark)**

   **(b)** Elena's white blood cells will help to fight the infection by engulfing and digesting the bacteria. Suggest **two** other ways that white blood cells help to defend the body. **(2 marks)**

   **(c)** Dave feels unwell. The doctor says he has influenza, which is caused by a virus. He tells Dave to take some paracetemol or aspirin. Why would the doctor suggest this? **(1 mark)**

**5.** Low carbohydrate, high protein diets are very popular with people wanting to lose weight. Scientists decided to investigate how the amount of protein in different diet plans affected the amount of weight lost.

This is what the scientists did.

- They found 100 obese people between 30 and 40 years of age and divided them into five equal groups.

- They gave each group a diet containing 1800 calories a day.

- They gave each group a different amount of protein in the diet plan. Similar foods were used for each group.

The average weight loss of each group after 26 weeks is shown in the bar chart below.

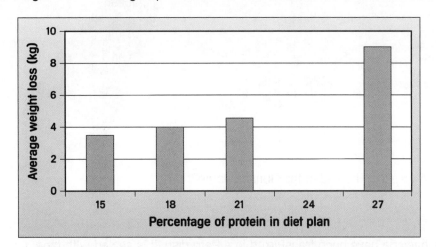

**(a)** The group with 24% protein lost an average of 6.5kg. Add this result to the chart.      (1 mark)

**(b)** Give **two** variables that the scientists tried to control in this experiment.      (2 marks)

_____

_____

**(c)** Suggest **two** variables that the scientists did not control.      (2 marks)

_____

_____

**(d)** What conclusion could you draw from this experiment?      (2 marks)

_____

_____

**6.** When scientists want to study bacteria in the laboratory, they grow them on a soft jelly-like substance.

**(a)** What is the name of this substance? (1 mark)

_____

**(b)** An inoculating loop is used to transfer bacteria. (1 mark)

Why is the wire loop heated in the Bunsen flame?

_____

**(c)** After the bacteria have been transferred to a Petri dish, it is sealed with tape.
Explain why. (2 marks)

_____

_____

**(d)** What is the maximum temperature used in school laboratories to incubate the cultures of bacteria?
Tick the correct answer. (1 mark)

**25°C** ☐          **32°C** ☐          **47°C** ☐

**7.** In March 2009 a nine-year-old girl was found to be infected with a new strain of the H1N1 swine flu virus. Over the next few weeks many more people were found to have the swine flu virus and in April 2009 the World Health Organisation declared a pandemic.

**(a)** Suggest how the new strain of the H1N1 virus arose. (2 marks)

_____

_____

**(b)** What do we mean by 'pandemic'? (1 mark)

_____

The graph below shows the number of reported cases of swine flu in the first ten days of May 2010.

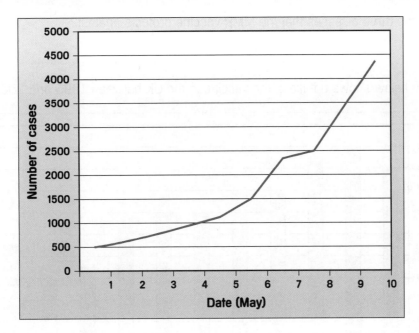

**(c)** How many cases of swine flu had been reported by 5th May?  (1 mark)

........................................................................

**(d)** Which period showed the largest increase in the number of reported cases?  (1 mark)

........................................................................

**(e)** Suggest why the spread of disease was so rapid.  (2 marks)

........................................................................

........................................................................

**(f)** Why is it difficult to kill viruses inside the body?  (2 marks)

........................................................................

........................................................................

**8.** Children are vaccinated against a range of diseases. Complete the sentences about vaccination.

Vaccines contain ............................................. pathogens. These stimulate the white blood cells to

produce ............................................. This results in the children becoming .............................................

to the disease.  (3 marks)

**9.** The MMR vaccine was introduced in the UK in 1995.

**(a)** What are the **three** diseases that the MMR vaccine protects against? (1 mark)

The graph below shows uptake of the vaccine in the UK between 1995 and 2007.

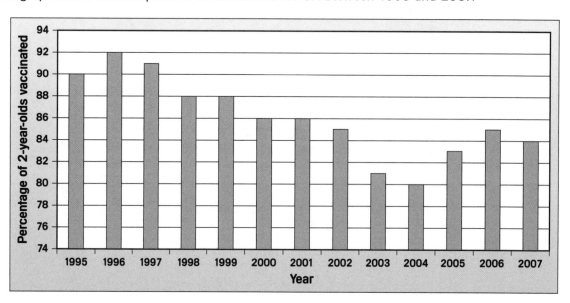

**(b)** What percentage of 2-year-olds was vaccinated in 2007? (1 mark)

**(c)** In which years was there a significant decline in uptake of the vaccine? (1 mark)

**(d)** Suggest a reason for the decline. (1 mark)

**10.** Complete the following sentences by underlining the correct words/phrases. (3 marks)

**(a)** A person is
| dehydrated |
| malnourished |
| anaemic |
if their diet is not balanced.

**(b)** A balanced diet should contain
| foods from each food group. |
| a mixture of fruit and carbohydrates. |
| no fatty foods. |

**(c)** Exercise will
| not affect |
| increase |
| decrease |
the amount of energy expended by the body.

**11.** Scientists often need to test bacteria for sensitivity to different antibiotics in order to decide the best antibiotic for treatment. To do this they spread the bacteria onto agar, which has been poured into a Petri dish and allowed to set. They then place small filter-paper discs containing different antibiotics onto the agar. The inoculated Petri dishes are incubated overnight and examined the following day.

**(a)** What is agar? (2 marks)

.................................................................................................................................................

.................................................................................................................................................

**(b)** The agar is heated to 121°C before it is poured into the Petri dish.

What is the reason for this? Underline the correct answer. (1 mark)

**So it pours easily**　　　**To dissolve the nutrients**　　　**To kill any microbes**

**(c)** Why are the inoculated Petri dishes incubated overnight? (1 mark)

.................................................................................................................................................

**(d)** The diagram below shows the Petri dish after incubation overnight.

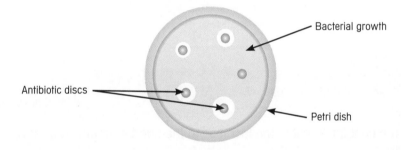

Erythromycin was found to be the most effective antibiotic. Penicillin had no effect at all on the bacteria.

**(i)** Label the antibiotic disc containing Erythromycin with an E. (1 mark)

**(ii)** Label the antibiotic disc containing Penicillin with a P. (1 mark)

**(Total:** ............. **/ 49 marks)**

12. Isoniazid was a drug developed in 1952 to treat tuberculosis (TB). Today one in seven new cases of TB is resistant to isoniazid.

    **(a)** Explain as fully as you can **one** way in which this resistance could have arisen.　　(4 marks)

    _____

    _____

    _____

    _____

    **(b)** Nowadays it is common practice to treat patients with TB using two different antibiotics simultaneously. Explain how this can help reduce antibiotic-resistant strains emerging.

    (2 marks)

    _____

    _____

    _____

    _____

    **(c)** Doctors are concerned about the increase in the number of MRSA (methicillin-resistant _Staphylococcus aureus_) infections they are seeing. What can doctors do to reduce the likelihood of resistant strains emerging?　　(2 marks)

    _____

    _____

    **(Total: ............ / 8 marks)**

1.  The body has receptors that respond to different stimuli. Complete the table below, matching the location of receptors to their stimuli. The first has been completed for you. (4 marks)

| Receptor | Stimulus |
|---|---|
| Eyes | Light |
| Nose | (a) |
| (b) | Sound |
| Skin | (c) |
| Skin | (d) |

2.  The diagram below shows a reflex action.

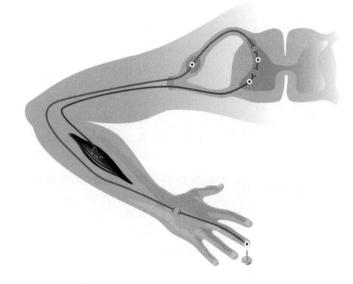

(a) Why does the body have reflex reactions? (1 mark)

(b) Draw **two** arrows on the diagram to show the direction of the nerve impulses along each of the neurones. (1 mark)

(c) There are three synapses on the diagram. Label any **two** of them with an 'S'. (1 mark)

(d) Explain what happens at a synapse. (4 marks)

**3.** Identify the parts of the nervous system shown on the diagram. (3 marks)

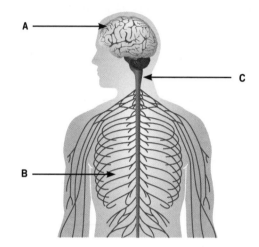

A ................................................................................................

B ................................................................................................

C ................................................................................................

**4.** The diagram shows a neurone.

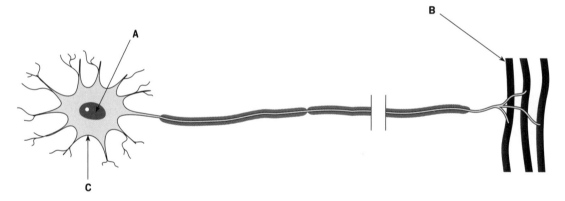

**(a)** Write the letter in the box that corresponds to the . . . (2 marks)

**(i)** Cell membrane

**(ii)** Nucleus

**(iii)** Effector

**(b)** What type of neurone is this? (1 mark)

**5.** The following sentences are about hormones. Underline the word or phrase that completes each sentence correctly. (4 marks)

Hormones are produced by

| |
|---|
| the brain. |
| white blood cells. |
| glands. |

They are transported to their target areas

| |
|---|
| by nerve cells. |
| in the blood. |
| attached to enzymes. |

A hormone used in the contraceptive pill is

| |
|---|
| follicle-stimulating hormone. |
| progesterone. |
| testosterone. |

A hormone given to women to increase fertility is

| |
|---|
| follicle-stimulating hormone. |
| progesterone. |
| testosterone. |

**6.** Matthew shines a torch into Jayna's eye. He notices that the pupil in her eye gets smaller.

**(a)** Complete the sentences about this reaction, choosing words from the box below. You may use the words once, more than once or not at all. (3 marks)

| eye | brain | nerves | light | reflex |
|---|---|---|---|---|

**(i)** The stimulus is the ............................................. .

**(ii)** The receptor is the ............................................. .

**(iii)** The response is carried out by the ............................................. .

**(b)** What type of reaction is this? (1 mark)

.................................................................................................................................

7. *In this question you will be assessed on using good English, organising information clearly and using specialist terms where appropriate.*

   A student germinated a bean seed. Diagram A shows the bean after seven days. She then turned the bean onto its side (diagram B). Diagram C shows the bean a week later.

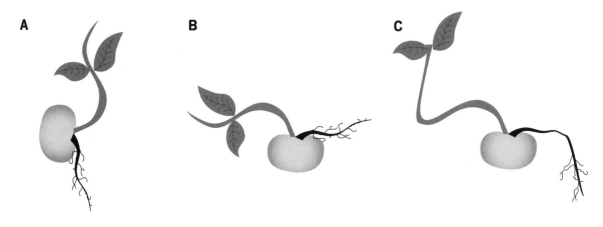

   A          B          C

   Explain fully why the plant responded in this way.       (3 marks)

8. Read the following passage about *in vitro* fertilisation (IVF).

   A woman unable to conceive may be offered IVF treatment. One cycle of treatment costs around £5000. Treatment involves numerous injections of fertility hormones so the woman will produce lots of eggs. Any spare eggs are destroyed. The success rate for one cycle of treatment is 28%. Doctors can now freeze spare eggs. If the first cycle of IVF is not successful, the frozen eggs can be thawed and used. Using frozen eggs costs around £1000 and reduces the need for repeated cycles of hormone therapy. Using frozen eggs has an 18% success rate. Some doctors are worried about the safety of using frozen eggs for the resulting children born, e.g. possible birth defects.

   **(a)** Give **two** advantages of using frozen eggs.       (2 marks)

   **(b)** Give **two** disadvantages of using frozen eggs.       (2 marks)

**9.** Ted uses 'ROOT-IT' to promote root growth in his plant cuttings. Bob makes his own rooting compound. He cuts some twigs of willow tree, mashes them into small pieces and leaves them to stand overnight in a tub of water. The next morning he removes the twigs and uses the water as rooting compound.

Ted and Bob want to know whose rooting compound is best. They take ten geranium cuttings each. They dip them in rooting compound and plant them. They measure the height of each cutting every four days. Their results are shown below.

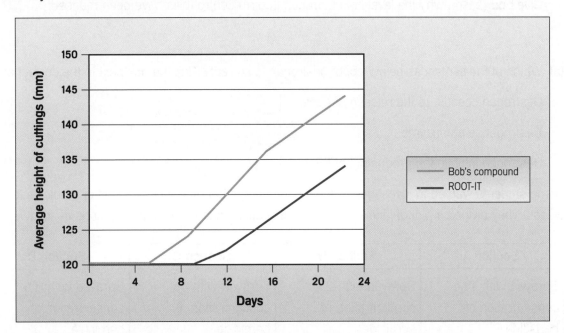

**(a)** Suggest **two** variables that Ted and Bob need to control to make the test fair. (2 marks)

_____

_____

**(b)** What conclusion could you draw from Bob and Ted's experiment? (2 marks)

_____

_____

**(c)** Suggest **one** disadvantage of using Bob's compound compared to ROOT-IT. (1 mark)

_____

**(d)** What is the substance present in both compounds that promotes root growth? (1 mark)

_____

**10.** The first contraceptive pills contained large amounts of oestrogen.

**(a)** Where in the body is oestrogen produced? (1 mark)

**(b)** Nowadays, birth control pills contain much lower doses of oestrogen, which is combined with progesterone. Some birth control pills contain progesterone only.

Give **one** reason why the levels of oestrogen in birth control pills have been reduced. (1 mark)

**(c)** Which of the sentences below about oestrogen is correct? Tick the box next to the correct answer.

Oestrogen speeds up the release of eggs.

Oestrogen is an enzyme.

Oestrogen inhibits the production of FSH. (1 mark)

**11.** Some students wanted to investigate the effect of using different concentrations of herbicide to kill weeds. They divided a plot of land into four equal sections and sprayed the sections as follows.

| Section A | Section B | Section C | Section D |
|---|---|---|---|
| Sprayed with 1% concentration of herbicide | Sprayed with 2% concentration of herbicide | Sprayed with 4% concentration of herbicide | Sprayed with 8% concentration of herbicide |

After a week the students counted the number of healthy weeds and dead weeds on each section. Their results are shown as pie charts.

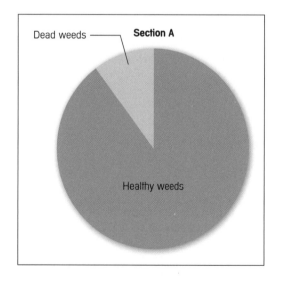

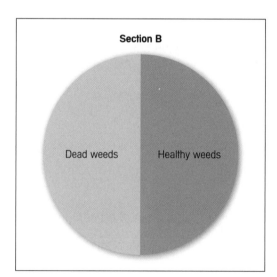

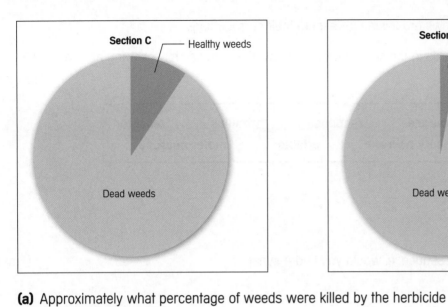

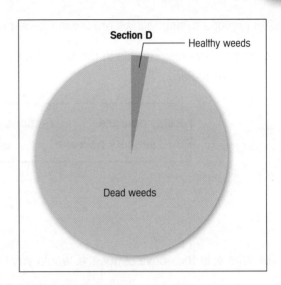

**(a)** Approximately what percentage of weeds were killed by the herbicide at 1% concentration? (1 mark)

**(b)** What concentration of herbicide killed most weeds? (1 mark)

**(c)** What concentration of herbicide would you recommend using? Explain your answer. (3 marks)

**(d)** Suggest **two** factors the students needed to control. (2 marks)

**(e)** Suggest a reason why weedkillers should not be used . . .

**(i)** to kill weeds growing at the edge of a pond. (1 mark)

**(ii)** to kill weeds in a hedgerow in the countryside. (1 mark)

**12.** The nervous system allows organisms to react to their surroundings.

**(a)** Put the following words in the correct order to show the pathway for receiving and responding to information. (3 marks)

| relay neurone | response | stimulus | receptor |
| sensory neurone | effector | motor neurone |

..............................................................................................................................................................

..............................................................................................................................................................

**(b)** Where, in the above sequence, would you find a synapse? (1 mark)

..............................................................................................................................................................

**13.** Which of the following statements about plants are true? Write the letters of the **four** TRUE statements in the boxes provided. (4 marks)

**A**  Plant shoots grow towards light.

**B**  Plant shoots grow towards moisture.

**C**  Roots have special cells called auxin cells.

**D**  Roots grow in the direction of gravity.

**E**  Plant auxins can be used as weedkillers.

**F**  Plant auxins can be used as medicine.

**G**  Geotropism is a response by the plant to the force of gravity.

|  |  |  |  |
|---|---|---|---|
|  |  |  |  |

**14.** It is important that the water and ion content of the body are controlled.

**(a)** Name the **two** ways that ions can be lost from the body. (2 marks)

................................................ and ................................................

**(b)** Name **one** other internal condition that must be controlled. (1 mark)

..............................................................................................................................................................

(Total: ............ / 61 marks)

1. Listed below are four types of drug.

    cannabis      alcohol      statins      aspirin

    Write the name of **one** drug from the list that is: (3 marks)

    **(a)** Illegal ..........................................................................................

    **(b)** Legal and prescribed ..................................................................

    **(c)** Legal and not prescribed ...........................................................

2. Complete the sentences below by filling in the missing words. (4 marks)

    Some athletes take ............................................ to enhance their performance. These drugs are

    ............................................ by most sporting bodies. They are made from the male hormone

    ............................................ . Misuse of these drugs may damage organs such as the

    ............................................ .

3. Some drugs are addictive.

    **(a)** Circle **two** drugs from the list below that are most addictive. (2 marks)

    nicotine      penicillin      aspirin      insulin      heroin

    **(b)** Explain why people who are addicted to a drug find it very difficult to stop taking the drug. (1 mark)

    ..............................................................................................................................................

    ..............................................................................................................................................

4. New drugs undergo testing before they are made available to the public. The steps below show the stages in drug development and testing BUT are in the wrong order.

    **(a)** Put the five stages in the correct order by placing the correct numbers in the boxes. Stage one has been done for you. (3 marks)

| | |
|---|---|
| Trials using low doses of the drug on a small number of healthy volunteers | |
| Drug is passed for use by general public | |
| New drug is made in the laboratory | 1 |
| Clinical trials involving large numbers of patients and volunteers | |
| Drug is tested in the laboratory using tissue culture | |

**(b)** Suggest **two** reasons why it is necessary for new drugs to undergo such testing. (2 marks)

.................................................................................................

.................................................................................................

**(c)** In clinical trials, one group of patients is often given a placebo.

**(i)** What is a placebo? (1 mark)

.................................................................................................

**(ii)** Explain why a placebo is given. (2 marks)

.................................................................................................

.................................................................................................

.................................................................................................

**5.** Read the following statements about cannabis:

Cannabis use has been linked to mental illness.

Cannabis can be used to treat the symptoms of a number of diseases.

Cannabis is not addictive.

Cannabis may act as a 'gateway' drug to more addictive drugs such as heroin and cocaine.

Cannabis smoke contains around 400 chemicals.

Smoking cannabis is less harmful than smoking cigarettes.

**(a)** Choose **two** statements that could be used to support an argument for cannabis to be made legal. (2 marks)

.................................................................................................

.................................................................................................

**(b)** Choose **two** statements that could be used to argue against cannabis being made legal. (2 marks)

.................................................................................................

.................................................................................................

**6.** American scientists have recently suggested that a statin pill could be given to people eating in fast food restaurants to offset the increased risk of heart disease caused by the fat in cheeseburgers, fries and milkshakes. They suggest that the cholesterol-lowering drug, which costs only a few pence, could be handed out along with sachets of tomato ketchup.

Suggest **two** reasons why some scientists think this is a bad idea. (2 marks)

.................................................................................................................................................................

.................................................................................................................................................................

**7.** Thalidomide is a drug that was developed as a sleeping pill. It was found to help relieve the symptoms of morning sickness in pregnant women.

Explain why it should not have been given to pregnant women to treat their morning sickness.

(2 marks)

.................................................................................................................................................................

.................................................................................................................................................................

**8.** Statins are drugs prescribed to lower cholesterol levels in the blood.

**(a)** Why is it important to lower cholesterol levels? (2 marks)

.................................................................................................................................................................

**(b)** What might happen to someone if a coronary artery becomes blocked? (1 mark)

.................................................................................................................................................................

**(c)** Which organ of the body do statins act on? Underline the correct answer. (1 mark)

**heart          pancreas          liver**

**9.** It is estimated that the cost to the NHS of treating people with smoking-related illnesses is more than £5 billion each year. The cost of treating people with illnesses related to illegal drug abuse is between £3 billion and £4 billion each year.

**(a)** Explain why the overall impact of smoking on health is greater than the impact of illegal drugs. (1 mark)

.................................................................................................................................................................

**(b)** Suggest **one** social impact of drug abuse. (1 mark)

.................................................................................................................................................................

**(c)** Suggest **one** economic impact of drug abuse. (1 mark)

.................................................................................................................................................................

(Total: ............. / 33 marks)

1. The illustration shows some adaptations of the polar bear.

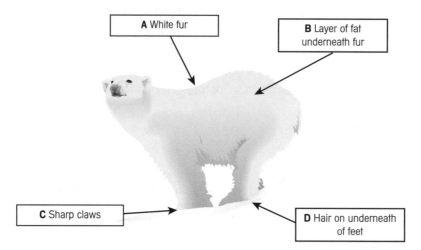

**A** White fur

**B** Layer of fat underneath fur

**C** Sharp claws

**D** Hair on underneath of feet

Match the adaptations to their functions by writing the correct letters (**A–D**) in the boxes below. (3 marks)

For catching seals ⬭

For warmth ⬭

To help grip the ice ⬭

For camouflage ⬭

2. The Fennec fox is found in the desert.

**(a)** Suggest how the fox's ears help it to survive in its environment. (1 mark)

_____

**(b)** The arctic fox is found in cold, snow-covered areas.

Suggest **one** difference (other than ears) between the Fennec fox and the arctic fox that helps each to survive in their different environments. (1 mark)

3. The photograph below shows a red-eyed tree frog. These frogs are bright green with red eyes, blue stripes and orange feet. They live in trees in the rainforest and feed on small insects.

Explain how each of the following adaptations helps the frog to survive.

**(a)** It has sticky pads on its 'fingers' and toes. (1 mark)

**(b)** When sleeping, it hides its bright colours by closing its eyes and tucking its feet beneath its body. (1 mark)

**(c)** It has a long, sticky tongue. (1 mark)

**4.** Gurjot and Ben wanted to investigate the effect of grazing on the numbers and types of plants in an area. They found a field grazed by horses and used a metre square quadrat.

Gurjot suggested they place five quadrats in the field as shown in the diagram right.

Ben said they should place the quadrats randomly.

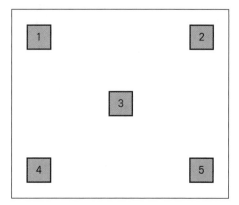

**(a)** Whose approach will give the most reliable results? (1 mark)

Gurjot and Ben counted the numbers of dandelion, dock and thistle plants inside each quadrat and found the mean average number of each type of plant per square metre. They repeated the experiment in another field grazed by sheep and a third field that had no animals grazing.

Their results are shown below.

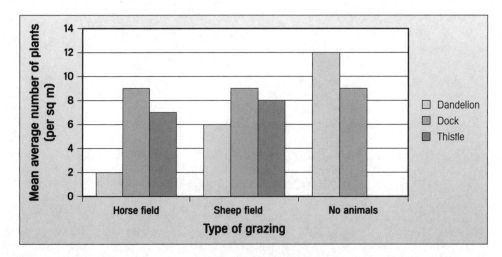

**(b)** The average mean number of thistles per square metre in the field with no animals was 7. Plot this result on the chart. (1 mark)

**(c)** Which field had the least number of dandelions? (1 mark)

**(d)** If the sheep field is 1000 square metres, calculate how many dandelion plants there are in the whole field. Show your working. (2 marks)

**(e)** What conclusions about the effect of grazing on plants could you draw from these results? (3 marks)

**(f)** Suggest **one** way in which Ben and Gurjot could improve the reliability of their results. (1 mark)

**(g)** Name **three** things that the dandelions, docks and thistles will compete with each other for. (3 marks)

5. The average daytime temperature in the Sahara desert is 45°C and it does not rain very often.

**(a)** Suggest **two** problems that animals living in the desert may have to deal with. (2 marks)

**(i)**

**(ii)**

**(b)** The cactus is a plant that is adapted to survive in desert environments.

Suggest how the following adaptations help the cactus to survive. (2 marks)

**(i)** The cactus has a thick stem.

**(ii)** The cactus has needles instead of leaves.

**6.** Scientists have discovered shrimps and giant worms that live clustered around hot vents on the ocean floor. These organisms can survive temperatures of up to 110°C. What name is given to such organisms? Underline the correct answer. (1 mark)

**mesophiles**     **gravophiles**     **extremophiles**

**7.** Dandelions, docks and thistles are all weeds and are well adapted to compete with other plants. The drawing below shows some features of a thistle.

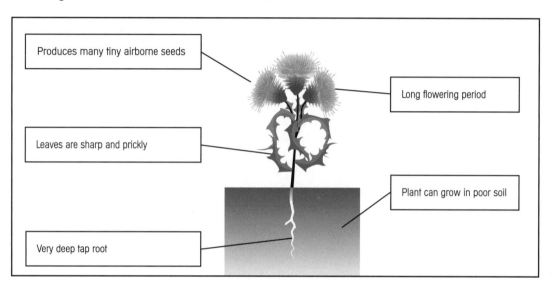

Produces many tiny airborne seeds

Long flowering period

Leaves are sharp and prickly

Plant can grow in poor soil

Very deep tap root

Choose any **three** of the above features. For each feature explain how it helps the thistle to compete and survive. (3 marks)

Feature 1: _____

_____

Feature 2: _____

_____

Feature 3: _____

_____

**8.** Complete the following paragraph about measuring environmental change by filling in the missing words. Choose words from the list below. (3 marks)

**oxygen    clean    polluted    indicator    gases    sewage    acid    microscopic**

Some invertebrate animals, such as the stonefly nymph, are found only in streams and rivers

where the water quality is high. These invertebrates are called _____

organisms. The rat-tailed maggot can survive in _____ water where the

levels of dissolved _____ are low.

**9.** Bird populations are a good indicator of environmental sustainability and allow scientists to track environmental changes in particular habitats.

Scientists measured the numbers of farmland birds and woodland birds in the UK between 1972 and 2002.

Their results are shown below.

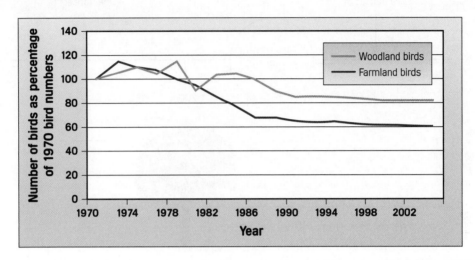

**(a)** Explain clearly how the numbers of farmland birds have changed between 1972 and 2002. (4 marks)

**(b)** Suggest a reason for the overall change in numbers of farmland birds. (1 mark)

**(c)** The government wants to reverse these changes by 2020. Suggest **one** thing it could do that would help to achieve this. (1 mark)

**10.** Suggest **two** factors that animals living in the same habitat will compete for. (2 marks)

11. Lichens are organisms that are sensitive to sulfur dioxide pollution.

Scientists wanted to investigate levels of pollution around an industrial area, so they carried out two line transects as shown on the diagram below. At 200-metre intervals along the transect they counted the number of lichens growing on the nearest tree, as shown in the diagram.

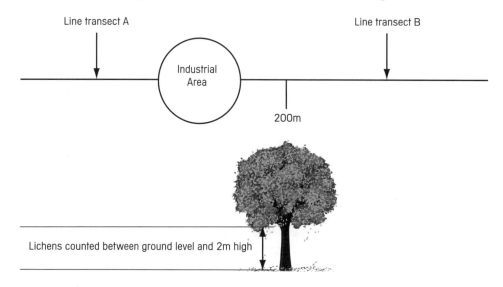

Line transect A

Line transect B

Industrial Area

200m

Lichens counted between ground level and 2m high

The number of lichens found are shown in the table.

| Transect | 200m | 400m | 600m | 800m | 1000m | 1200m | 1400m | 1600m |
|---|---|---|---|---|---|---|---|---|
| A | 0 | 0 | 3 | 4 | 5 | 8 | 9 | 8 |
| B | 2 | 5 | 8 | 9 | 9 | 7 | 8 | 9 |

**(a)** Suggest why the results for the two transects are different. (1 mark)

_____

**(b)** What conclusion could you draw from the results of line transect A? (1 mark)

_____

**(c)** Suggest why scientists did not count the number of lichens on the whole tree. (2 marks)

_____

_____

**(d)** Suggest **one** factor scientists were unable to control that could affect the reliability of the results. (1 mark)

_____

**(Total:** _____ **/ 44 marks)**

1. In an area of marshland there are numerous plants that are eaten by insects. The insects are eaten by frogs. Herons eat the frogs.

**(a)** Complete the pyramid of biomass by writing the names of the organisms in the correct places. (3 marks)

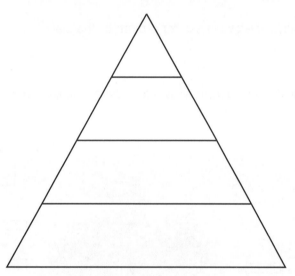

**(b)** What is the source of energy for all of the organisms in the marshland? (1 mark)

_____

**(c)** Why is the biomass at each stage of the food chain less than the biomass of the previous stage? (1 mark)

_____

_____

**(d)** A farmer sprays a nearby field with pesticide. Some of the spray falls on the marshland and kills the insects. How will this affect the number of frogs?

Explain your answer. (2 marks)

_____

_____

**2.** The drawing below shows energy transfer in photosynthesis.

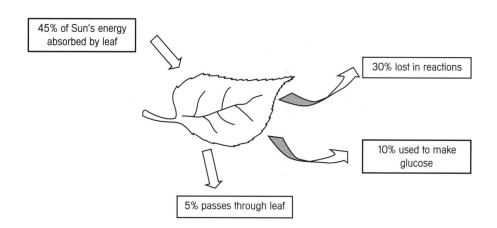

**(a)** How much of the Sun's energy is used for growth by the leaf? (1 mark)

........................................................................................................................................................

**(b)** A squirrel eats the leaf. The diagram shows the energy intake and output of the squirrel.

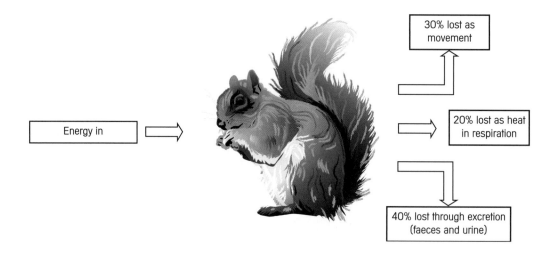

What percentage of the squirrel's energy intake is used for growth? (1 mark)

........................................................................................................................................................

**(c)** Use your answers from parts **(a)** and **(b)** to calculate what percentage of the Sun's energy is used by the squirrel for growth. Show your working out. (2 marks)

.................................................................................................................................................................

.................................................................................................................................................................

**(d)** Suggest why it is more energy efficient to have a vegetarian diet. (2 marks)

.................................................................................................................................................................

.................................................................................................................................................................

**3.** The diagram below shows a food web for some animals that live on an allotment.

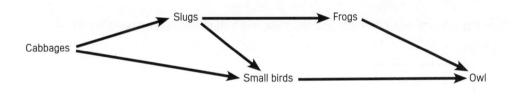

Suggest **three** reasons why only a small amount of the Sun's energy captured by the cabbage will be available to the owl. (3 marks)

.................................................................................................................................................................

.................................................................................................................................................................

.................................................................................................................................................................

**(Total: ............ / 16 marks)**

# B1 Waste Materials from Plants and Animals

**1.** Many people recycle their garden waste to make compost. This can be used to provide nutrients for growing plants.

**(a)** The following list contains substances that can be recycled. Put a tick next to the **three** substances that could be put in the compost heap. (3 marks)

Glass ☐

Teabags ☐

Grass cuttings ☐

Tin cans ☐

Vegetable peelings ☐

Cooked meat ☐

**2.** Underline the correct word in each box below to complete the sentences about the carbon cycle. (4 marks)

Plants and [ animals / algae / fungi ] remove carbon dioxide from the air.

Plants use the carbon obtained to produce [ glucose. / nitrates. / minerals. ]

When plants die, they are broken down by [ consumers. / decomposers. / producers. ]

Bacteria and fungi are examples of [ consumers. / decomposers. / producers. ]

**3.** Jim, Robert and Harriet are all keen gardeners.
They make their own compost by collecting leaves from the garden and putting them in a heap.
Jim and Robert cover their heaps with thick black plastic to absorb the heat from the Sun.

Their compost heaps are shown below.

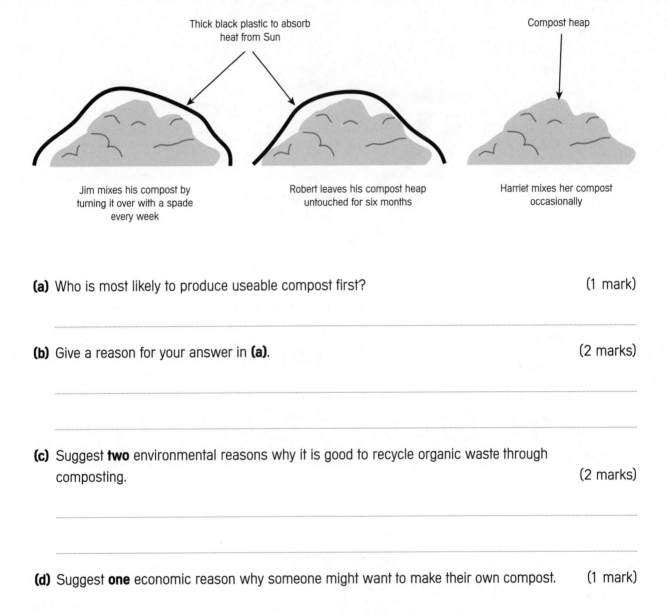

Thick black plastic to absorb
heat from Sun

Compost heap

Jim mixes his compost by
turning it over with a spade
every week

Robert leaves his compost heap
untouched for six months

Harriet mixes her compost
occasionally

**(a)** Who is most likely to produce useable compost first? (1 mark)

........................................................................................................................................

**(b)** Give a reason for your answer in **(a)**. (2 marks)

........................................................................................................................................

........................................................................................................................................

**(c)** Suggest **two** environmental reasons why it is good to recycle organic waste through
composting. (2 marks)

........................................................................................................................................

........................................................................................................................................

**(d)** Suggest **one** economic reason why someone might want to make their own compost. (1 mark)

........................................................................................................................................

4.  The diagram below shows some parts of the carbon cycle.

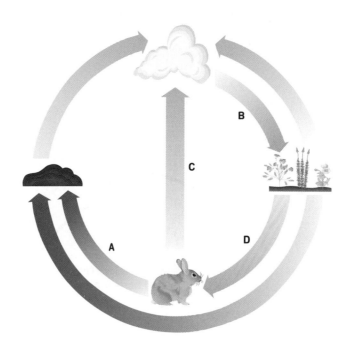

**(a)** Choose the letters from the diagram that correspond to the following processes:     (4 marks)

Feeding       ☐

Excretion     ☐

Photosynthesis ☐

Respiration   ☐

**(b)** Name another process, not shown on the diagram, that releases carbon dioxide into the air.     (1 mark)

....................................................................................................................................................

**5.** A group of students wanted to investigate factors affecting decay.
They mixed some soil with some small discs cut from leaves.

They divided the leaf disc/soil mixture equally into four test tubes as shown below.

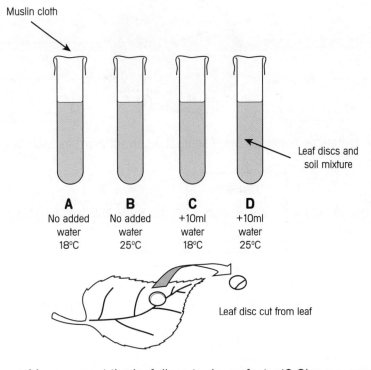

Muslin cloth

Leaf discs and
soil mixture

| **A** | **B** | **C** | **D** |
| No added | No added | +10ml | +10ml |
| water | water | water | water |
| 18°C | 25°C | 18°C | 25°C |

Leaf disc cut from leaf

**(a)** In which tube would you expect the leaf discs to decay fastest? Give a reason for your answer. (2 marks)

**(b)** The students did not add any microorganisms to the test tubes. Where will the microorganisms that cause decay come from? (1 mark)

**(c)** Why did the students seal the tubes with muslin cloth instead of a rubber bung? (1 mark)

**(d)** Suggest **one** way in which the students could use the leaf discs to measure the rate of decay. (1 mark)

**(Total: ........... / 23 marks)**

**1.** **(a)** Use the following words to label the cell below. (4 marks)

chromosomes      nucleus      cytoplasm      cell membrane

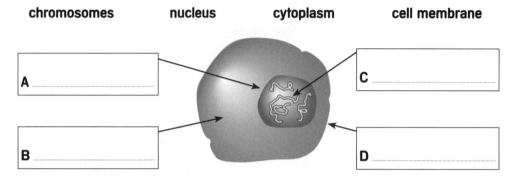

A ..................................................

B ..................................................

C ..................................................

D ..................................................

**(b)** Complete the sentences below by underlining the correct word in each box below. (3 marks)

Sexual reproduction is the ⎡ division / separation / fusion ⎤ of the male and female gametes.

The resulting offspring will contain ⎡ DNA / cells / enzymes ⎤ from both parents.

This gives rise to ⎡ fertilisation. / differentiation. / variation. ⎤

**2.** Below are some statements about genes. Some are correct and some are incorrect. Write the letters of the **three** correct statements in the boxes below. (3 marks)

**A** Genes are sections of DNA.

**B** Genes can code for proteins.

**C** A sperm cell has 23 genes.

**D** Genes are found in the cytoplasm of cells.

**E** Genes are transferred to offspring only in sexual reproduction.

**F** Chromosomes contain many genes.

|  |  |  |
|---|---|---|
|  |  |  |

**3.** Variation can be due to inherited factors, environmental factors, or a combination of both. Cathy and Drew are sister and brother.

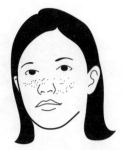 

The table below shows how they are different.

For each difference, complete the table to show if the difference is caused by inherited factors **(I)**, environmental factors **(E)**, or a combination of both **(B)**. (4 marks)

| Cathy | Drew | Inherited (I), environmental (E), or both (B) |
|---|---|---|
| Freckles | No freckles | **(a)** |
| Long hair | Short hair | **(b)** |
| Good at music | Good at sport | **(c)** |
| Not colour blind | Colour blind | **(d)** |

**4.** The diagram below shows the first stage in the process of insulin production using genetic engineering.

**(a)** What do scientists use to 'cut out' the insulin gene from the chromosome? (1 mark)

**(b)** The 'cut' gene is then inserted into a bacterium. Why are bacteria good host cells for the 'cut' insulin gene? (2 marks)

**5.** The diagram below shows the sequence of events used to clone sheep by embryo transplantation.

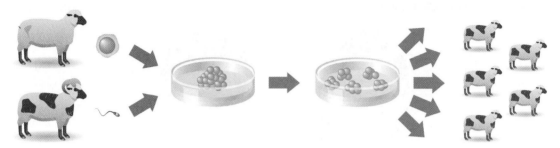

**(a)** Use words from the box to complete the sentences below. (5 marks)

| gametes | old | implanted | shocked |
|---|---|---|---|
| directed | characteristics | sexual | wombs |
| asexual | sterile | stomachs | specialised |

A male and female sheep with the desired _____ are mated. This is an

example of _____ reproduction. The embryo is removed from the female

before the cells become _____. The embryo is split into several clumps

which are then _____ into the _____ of surrogate sheep.

**(b)** Why would farmers want to use embryo transplants rather than waiting for the original
female sheep to give birth? (2 marks)

_____

_____

_____

**(c)** Explain why the offspring from the above process will be identical to each other but not
identical to the parents. (4 marks)

_____

_____

_____

_____

**(d)** Scientists now have the technology to clone human embryos.
Give **one** medical reason why cloning human embryos might be allowed. (1 mark)

_____

_____

**6.** GM crops are made by cutting out desired genes from one plant and inserting them into another plant. Read the following statements about GM crops.

- GM crops give higher yields.

- GM crops might breed with wild plants.

- GM crops are insect resistant, thus reducing use of pesticides.

- GM crops can be enriched with nutrients, so are more healthy.

- GM crops may harm insects that feed on them.

- GM crops take up less land, leaving more for wildlife.

**(a)** Using the information above, suggest **three** reasons that could be used to support the development of GM crops.                                                                                                (3 marks)

......................................................................................................................................................

......................................................................................................................................................

......................................................................................................................................................

**(b)** Suggest **two** reasons why people are against the growing of GM crops.                    (2 marks)

......................................................................................................................................................

......................................................................................................................................................

**(c)** Suggest **one** reason (not mentioned above) why scientists have developed GM crops.        (1 mark)

......................................................................................................................................................

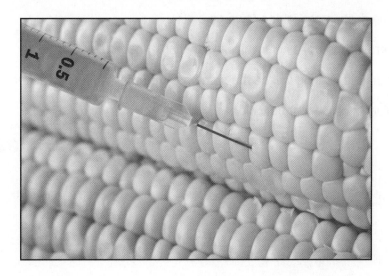

**7.** Adult cell cloning can be used to produce individuals with desired characteristics, e.g. good beef production in cows.

**(a)** The instructions below indicate the stages in adult cell cloning, but are in the wrong order. Put them in the correct order by numbering them 1–6. Two have been done for you. **(3 marks)**

The nucleus is removed from the egg cell. ⬜

The embryo is implanted in the womb of another cow. ⬜

The egg cell is fused with the body cell. ⬜

A body cell is taken from a prize bull. ⬜

The fused cells start to divide to form an embryo. **5**

An unfertilised egg cell is taken from cow B. **2**

**(b)** At stage 5, how are the cells prompted to divide? **(1 mark)**

---

**8.** Spider plants reproduce by producing stolons. This is an example of asexual reproduction.

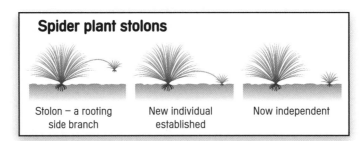

**Spider plant stolons**

Stolon – a rooting side branch

New individual established

Now independent

Circle the correct word from the pair given in the sentences below. **(4 marks)**

**(a)** Asexual reproduction needs **one / two** parent(s).

**(b)** Asexual reproduction does not involve production of **gametes / DNA**.

**(c)** The genes in the offspring will be **the same as / different to** the parent genes.

**(d)** The new plant is called a **shoot / clone**.

**(Total: ........... / 43 marks)**

**1.** Many years ago, members of the giraffe family had short necks. The scientist Charles Darwin had some ideas about how organisms evolved. His theory suggested that some giraffes were born with longer necks, which gave them an advantage in finding food. They were therefore more successful and were able to breed and pass on their 'long neck' to their offspring.

Lamarck was another scientist with ideas about evolution. He had a theory that some giraffes grew longer necks to reach the leaves high on the trees. These giraffes were then more successful and were able to breed and pass their 'long necks' onto their offspring.

**(a)** Explain why Lamarck's theory is not correct. (2 marks)

......................................................................................................................................................

......................................................................................................................................................

......................................................................................................................................................

**(b)** Darwin also suggested that humans and apes evolved from a common ancestor. Give **two** reasons why Darwin's theories were not accepted by some people. (2 marks)

......................................................................................................................................................

......................................................................................................................................................

**(c)** How many years would it take for the short-necked giraffes to evolve into the modern giraffes of today? Underline the best answer. (1 mark)

**five thousand**          **five hundred thousand**          **five million**

2.  The diagram below shows an evolutionary tree for some of our present-day vertebrates.

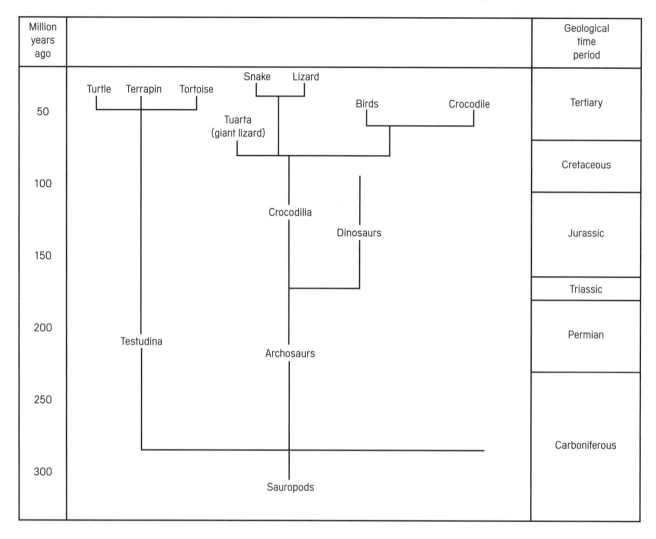

**(a)** How many millions of years ago did the testudina appear? (1 mark)

..........................................................................................................................................................................

**(b)** In what geological time period did the dinosaurs become extinct? (1 mark)

..........................................................................................................................................................................

**(c)** How do scientists know that dinosaurs once lived on Earth? (1 mark)

..........................................................................................................................................................................

**(d)** What group of animals alive today is most closely related to the snake? (1 mark)

..........................................................................................................................................................................

**(e)** Which ancestor is shared by dinosaurs, crocodiles and the giant lizard, but is not an ancestor of tortoises? (1 mark)

..........................................................................................................................................................................

**3.** Which of these passages describes the Theory of Evolution?
Tick the best answer. (1 mark)

Most species have been around since the Earth was first formed and
have changed to adapt to changes in the environment. ☐

Animals developed from insects approximately 200 million years ago.
Plants developed from organisms in the sea. ☐

All species in existence have developed from simple life forms
over a period of approximately 3 billion years. ☐

**4.** *In this question you will be assessed on using good English, organising information clearly and using specialist terms where appropriate.*

Describe Darwin's theory of evolution by natural selection. (6 marks)

.....................................................................................................................................................................

.....................................................................................................................................................................

.....................................................................................................................................................................

.....................................................................................................................................................................

.....................................................................................................................................................................

**5.**

Marsupials are a group of mammals that carry their young in the early stages of infancy in a pouch. The kangaroo and koala bear are examples of marsupials and yet they are very different. The koala bear spends much of its time climbing trees and has five fingers with short claws that grip the tree trunks. It spends up to 18 hours a day sleeping and is a solitary animal. Kangaroos are much more sociable and are found in herds. They have powerful hind legs and large back feet for jumping.

Scientists in Australia have recently discovered 26 fossils of an animal they believe lived 15 million years ago. The creature, which they have named Nimbaden, was about the size of a sheep with giant claws. The fact that so many fossils were found in one place suggests that Nimbaden may have travelled in herds. Some of the skulls found were of babies still in their mothers' pouches.

**(a)** Scientists believe that Nimbaden was a marsupial. Why do they think this?          (1 mark)

.................................................................................................................................................................

.................................................................................................................................................................

**(b)** What fact suggests that Nimbaden may have been related to modern-day koala bears?     (1 mark)

.................................................................................................................................................................

**(c)** In what way do scientists think Nimbaden was like modern-day kangaroos?          (1 mark)

.................................................................................................................................................................

**(d)** What term do we use to describe animals that lived millions of years ago but no longer exist?  (1 mark)

.................................................................................................................................................................

**6.** Scientists frequently study the distribution of the common snail, Cepaea. The snail has a shell that can be brown or yellow, and striped or unstriped. The shell colour and banding influences the visibility of snails to thrushes that prey on them. A recent study compared the distribution of snails in forest and countryside areas. The results, as a percentage, are shown below.

| Area | Striped shell (%) | Unstriped shell (%) |
|---|---|---|
| Forest / woodland | 13 | 87 |
| Open countryside / hedgerows | 75 | 25 |

**(a)** Suggest a reason for this distribution of snails. (2 marks)

.................................................................................................................................................................

.................................................................................................................................................................

**(b)** Which colour shelled snail would you expect to find most of in forest / woodland areas? Explain your answer. (2 marks)

.................................................................................................................................................................

.................................................................................................................................................................

Scientists also believe that shell colour influences the body temperature of the snails. Snails with dark shells warm up faster than those with light shells.

In cold areas, this would be advantageous to the dark-coloured snail.

The average annual temperature in Scotland is 2°C lower than in England.

**(c)** Where would you expect to find the highest percentage of snails with brown shells? (1 mark)

.................................................................................................................................................................

**(d)** Suggest what may happen to the numbers of brown and yellow-shelled snails if our climate continues to get hotter due to global warming. Give a reason for your answer. (2 marks)

.................................................................................................................................................................

.................................................................................................................................................................

**(Total: ............ / 28 marks)**

1.  Atoms are the fundamental building blocks of the things we see around us.          (4 marks)

    Label the diagram of an atom below. Use the following words: **nucleus, proton, neutron, electron**.

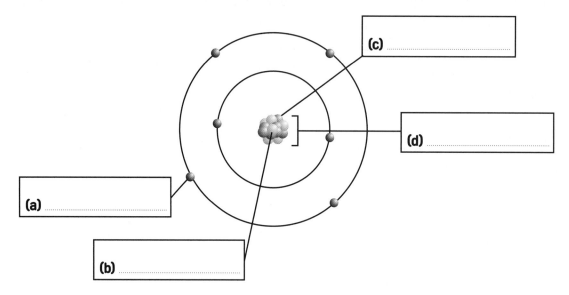

(c) ........................................

(d) ........................................

(a) ........................................

(b) ........................................

2.  **(a)** What is meant by the term **element**? How many elements are there?          (2 marks)

    ....................................................................................................................

    ....................................................................................................................

    **(b)** Where and how are elements grouped together?          (2 marks)

    ....................................................................................................................

    ....................................................................................................................

    **(c)** Use the Periodic Table to find the chemical symbols for these elements:          (3 marks)

    Fluorine: ..........................................

    Silicon: ..........................................

    Tungsten: ..........................................

3.  **(a)** Explain what is meant by the term compound.          (2 marks)

    ....................................................................................................................

    ....................................................................................................................

    **(b)** What types of chemical bonds can atoms make when elements react with each other?          (2 marks)

    ....................................................................................................................

    ....................................................................................................................

**4.** **(a)** What does the chemical formula of a compound show? Use the words **atoms** and **elements** in your answer. (2 marks)

........................................................................................................................................................

........................................................................................................................................................

**(b)** Use mathematical functions and insert brackets to show what the following chemical formulae mean. The first one has been completed for you. (3 marks)

$MgCl_2 = (1 \times Mg) + (2 \times Cl)$

**(i)** $2H_2O$ ........................................................

**(ii)** 2NaOH ........................................................

**(iii)** $Mg(OH)_2$ ........................................................

**(c)** Complete the table by filling in the spaces to show the number of molecules and the number of each atom in each compound. The first one has been done for you. (6 marks)

| Chemical formula | Number of molecules | Number of atoms |
|---|---|---|
| 2MgO | 2 | $2(1 \times Mg) = 2 \times Mg$ <br> $2(1 \times O) = 2 \times O$ |
| $2Al_2O_3$ | **(i)** ............... | **(ii)** ............... ............... |
| $HNO_3$ | **(iii)** ............... | **(iv)** ............... ............... |
| $3Fe_2O_3$ | **(v)** ............... | **(vi)** ............... ............... |

**5.** **(a)** When you write a word equation, what are the **reactants** and **products**? (2 marks)

**(i)** Reactants: ........................................................

**(ii)** Products: ........................................................

**(b)** Label the **reactants** and the **products** in the following reaction: (2 marks)

**sodium + chlorine**  **sodium chloride**

........................................................................................................................................................

**6.** What has to happen for a chemical equation to be balanced? (2 marks)

....................................................................................................................................

....................................................................................................................................

**7.** **(a)** Complete the table by writing down the word equation for the reaction shown below. (3 marks)

| Reactants | | | → | Products |
|---|---|---|---|---|
| .......... | + | .......... | → | .......... |
| Mg | + | $O_2$ | → | MgO |

**(b)** Use the diagram below to explain how you would balance the equation. (2 marks)

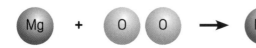

....................................................................................................................................

....................................................................................................................................

**8.** Draw lines to match up the pictures with the correct labels. (3 marks)

**(a)**

| A solid | | A compound |

**(b)**
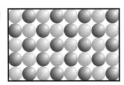

| A liquid | | An element |

**(c)**
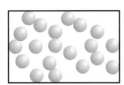

| A gas | | A compound |

**9.** Read the following statements and write word equations for them.
When you have completed them, go back and write the balanced symbol equations.
Then underline the **reactants** and circle the **products** for both word and symbol equations.

**(a)** When hydrogen ($H_2$) reacts with oxygen ($O_2$), water ($H_2O$) is produced. (2 marks)

**(b)** In the thermite reaction, aluminium powder (Al) reacts with iron (III) oxide ($Fe_2O_3$). The products are aluminium oxide ($Al_2O_3$) and liquid iron (Fe). (2 marks)

**(c)** Petrol is mostly a compound called octane ($C_8H_{18}$). When it burns completely in oxygen ($O_2$), the products are carbon dioxide ($CO_2$) and water ($H_2O$). (2 marks)

**(d)** In the reaction of sodium (Na) with water ($H_2O$), the products are an alkaline solution of sodium hydroxide (NaOH) and the gas hydrogen ($H_2$), which burns with a yellow flame due to the sodium ions. (2 marks)

**(e)** Sodium chloride (NaCl) and water ($H_2O$) are produced when hydrochloric acid (HCl) is neutralised by sodium hydroxide (NaOH). (2 marks)

**(f)** Hydrogen peroxide ($H_2O_2$) decomposes over time to form water ($H_2O$) and oxygen gas ($O_2$). (2 marks)

**10.** Are the following statements true or false? Write **True** or **False** next to each statement.

**(a)** Iron contains only one type of atom. _____ (1 mark)

**(b)** There are more non-metal elements than metallic elements. _____ (1 mark)

**(c)** All elements are solids at room temperature. _____ (1 mark)

**(d)** An apple is an element. _____ (1 mark)

**(e)** Mercury and bromine are liquids at room temperature. _____ (1 mark)

**(f)** Water is an element; it is made up of hydrogen and

oxygen atoms. _____ (1 mark)

**(g)** The majority of carbon atoms in your body have been on Earth since it was

first formed. _____ (1 mark)

**(h)** All gases are elements. _____ (1 mark)

**(i)** Wood is a compound. _____ (1 mark)

**(j)** The symbol for sodium is So. _____ (1 mark)

**(k)** All metals are elements. _____ (1 mark)

**(l)** Compounds always contain different types of atoms. _____ (1 mark)

**(m)** Everything on Earth is made of atoms. _____ (1 mark)

**(n)** Lead atoms are heavier than helium atoms. _____ (1 mark)

**(o)** There are about 1000 different elements in existence. _____ (1 mark)

**11.** Write the correct answers at the end of the following sentences. (5 marks)

**(a)** A compound of this metal is essential for strong teeth. _____

**(b)** A gas that gives a 'squeaky pop' with a lighted splint. _____

**(c)** Metal that reacts with water, burning with a lilac flame. _____

**(d)** Metal used in fireworks. Burns with a bright, white flame. _____

**(e)** A solid, yellow non-metal. Burns to make an acidic gas. _____

**(Total:** _____ **/ 72 marks)**

**1.** Limestone can be used to make several useful products.

**(a)** (Circle) **two** words below that are useful products made from limestone. (2 marks)

    **cement**       **diesel**       **glass**       **petrol**       **plastic**

**(b)** What is the main chemical compound in limestone? (1 mark)

_____

**2.** Daniel did an experiment to investigate the properties of limestone.

He heated a piece of limestone very strongly as shown in the diagram.

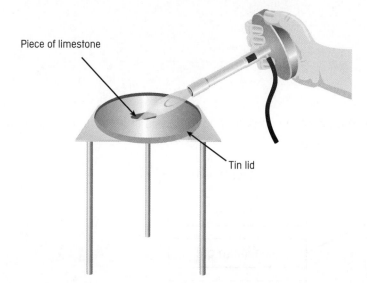

Piece of limestone

Tin lid

**(a)** He found that when limestone is heated it forms two products, a white powder and a gas.
Complete the word equation for the experiment by selecting the correct product from the list.

    **calcium carbide**       **calcium hydroxide**       **calcium nitride**       **calcium oxide**

calcium carbonate $\xrightarrow{\text{heat}}$ _____ + carbon dioxide (1 mark)

**(b)** Slaked lime (calcium hydroxide) is a useful product that can be made by reacting calcium oxide (quicklime) with water.

Write a word equation for this reaction. (1 mark)

_____

**(c)** Slaked lime is used to neutralise acidic soils. What does the term **neutralise** mean? (1 mark)

_____

**3.** **(a)** Describe the process in which limestone is used to make glass. (2 marks)

......................................................................................................................................................

......................................................................................................................................................

**(b)** Briefly describe the process of producing cement. (1 mark)

......................................................................................................................................................

**(c)** Cement is one of the raw materials used to make concrete. Which **three** other materials are also required? (3 marks)

**(i)** ..............................................................................................

**(ii)** ..............................................................................................

**(iii)** ..............................................................................................

**4.** Draw a line to match each of the construction materials in list A to what it is made from in list B. The first one has been done for you. (4 marks)

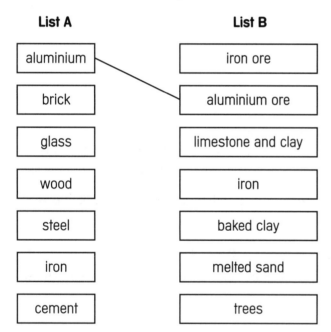

| List A | List B |
| --- | --- |
| aluminium | iron ore |
| brick | aluminium ore |
| glass | limestone and clay |
| wood | iron |
| steel | baked clay |
| iron | melted sand |
| cement | trees |

**5.** Fill in the empty boxes in the table below to show the **four** main uses of limestone and how it is obtained. (5 marks)

| Use | How it is obtained/made |
|---|---|
| **(a)** _____ | Quarried and cut into blocks. |
| Neutralising agent | **(b)** _____ |
| **(c)** _____ | Mix limestone, sand and sodium carbonate, and then heat the mixture until it melts. When cool it is transparent. |
| **(d)** _____ | **(e)** _____ |

**6.** Although limestone is an important raw material, the way in which it is extracted and used has an impact on the environment, people and the economy.

**(a)** Give two **advantages** of quarrying limestone to produce construction materials. (2 marks)

_____

_____

**(b)** Give two **disadvantages** of quarrying limestone to produce construction materials. (2 marks)

_____

_____

**(c)** Choose **one** of the disadvantages you gave in part **(b)** and briefly describe its effects and consequences. (3 marks)

_____

_____

_____

_____

_____

**7.** **(a)** Complete the table by writing down **one advantage** and **one disadvantage** of using limestone, concrete and glass as construction materials.

| Material | Advantage | Disadvantage | |
|---|---|---|---|
| Limestone | **(i)** | **(ii)** | (1 mark) |
| Concrete | **(iii)** | **(iv)** | (1 mark) |
| Glass | **(v)** | **(vi)** | (1 mark) |

**(b)** Why are these materials often a more suitable choice for construction than wood?　(2 marks)

**8.** This question is about construction materials.

**(a)** Look at this picture. It shows a building being constructed using reinforced concrete.

Reinforced concrete is a composite material containing steel rods and concrete.

Reinforced concrete is a better construction material than non-reinforced concrete.

Explain why. Use ideas about the properties of concrete and steel.　(2 marks)

**(b)** Some construction materials are made from rocks in the Earth's crust.

Iron, brick and glass are construction materials.

Draw straight lines to link each construction material in list A to the rock it is made from in list B.

(3 marks)

| List A | List B |
|--------|--------|
| iron | haematite ore |
| brick | sand |
| glass | baked clay |

(Total: _____ / 38 marks)

**1.** What is an ore? (1 mark)

**2.** The method used for extracting a metal depends on how reactive it is.

**(a)** Give the name of **one** unreactive metal and describe briefly how it is obtained. (2 marks)

**(b)** Describe how a metal can be extracted from its oxide. (1 mark)

**(c)** What is the chemical name for this process? (1 mark)

**(d)** How are metals that are less reactive than carbon extracted from their ores? (1 mark)

**3.** **(a)** What does molten iron contain? (1 mark)

**(b)** How can the properties of iron be changed? (1 mark)

**(c)** State **one** common alloy made from iron. (1 mark)

**4.** **(a)** Explain what is meant by the term **alloy**. (1 mark)

**(b)** Why are alloys usually stronger and harder than the pure metals used to make them? (2 marks)

**5.** Draw a line to match each type of alloy in list A to its use in list B. The first one has been done for you.

(3 marks)

**List A**                    **List B**

| aluminium alloy is strong and lightweight | general construction |
| brass helps kill some bacteria | aeroplanes |
| normal steel is strong and cheap | statues |
| solder has a low melting point | knives and forks |
| stainless steel is strong and will not rust | hospital door handles |
| bronze is easy to cast into shapes | sticking metals together |

**6.** How is steel made? Briefly describe the main points in the process. (3 marks)

.................................................................................................................................

.................................................................................................................................

.................................................................................................................................

.................................................................................................................................

**7.** Complete the table to show how the properties of steel are affected by the elements that are added to it.

(4 marks)

| Type of steel | Properties | Example of use |
|---|---|---|
| **(a)** ................... | Hard and strong | Cutting tools |
| Low carbon steel | **(b)** ................... | Car body panels |
| **(c)** ................... | Resistant to corrosion | **(d)** ................... |

**8.** Titanium is a transition metal with many useful properties. It is used to make replacement joints, such as hip joints, for people whose bones have worn out. Summer County NHS Trust wants to save money by replacing expensive titanium hip joints with cheap aluminium ones. Why is this a bad idea and why is titanium more suitable? (3 marks)

.................................................................................................................................

.................................................................................................................................

.................................................................................................................................

9. **(a)** The elements in the central block of the Periodic Table are known as the transition metals. Write down the names of **three** of these elements. (3 marks)

(i) .......................................................................................................................................

(ii) .......................................................................................................................................

(iii) .......................................................................................................................................

**(b)** Transition metals are often used as structural materials and as electrical and thermal conductors. List **three** reasons why they are suitable for these uses. (3 marks)

(i) .......................................................................................................................................

(ii) .......................................................................................................................................

(iii) .......................................................................................................................................

10. **(a)** What is the name of the process that is used to extract aluminium, copper and titanium? (1 mark)

.......................................................................................................................................

**(b)** Why is it important to recycle metals? List **three** reasons. (3 marks)

(i) .......................................................................................................................................

(ii) .......................................................................................................................................

(iii) .......................................................................................................................................

11. The metal frame of these glasses is made from a smart alloy called nitinol. This alloy is made from nickel and titanium.

Give **one** advantage of making the frame from a smart alloy, instead of an ordinary metal. (2 marks)

.......................................................................................................................................

.......................................................................................................................................

.......................................................................................................................................

**(Total: ............ / 37 marks)**

1.  Crude oil is a mixture of compounds called hydrocarbons.

    **(a)** What is a hydrocarbon?                                                                                      (1 mark)

    .................................................................................................................................................

    **(b)** What is the name of the process by which crude oil is separated into its useful parts?      (1 mark)

    .................................................................................................................................................

    **(c)** Explain why crude oil can be separated in this way. Use ideas about boiling point, molecular size and intermolecular forces in your answer.                                                                      (2 marks)

    .................................................................................................................................................

    .................................................................................................................................................

    .................................................................................................................................................

2.  **Pentane** is an **alkane** that has the formula $C_5H_{12}$. A molecule of pentane can be represented as shown:

$$
\begin{array}{ccccccccc}
 & H & & H & & H & & H & & H \\
 & | & & | & & | & & | & & | \\
H- & C & - & C & - & C & - & C & - & C & -H \\
 & | & & | & & | & & | & & | \\
 & H & & H & & H & & H & & H \\
\end{array}
$$

    **(a)** What do the letters C and H represent?                                                                 (1 mark)

    .................................................................................................................................................

    **(b)** What do the lines between each C and H represent?                                              (1 mark)

    .................................................................................................................................................

    **(c)** The hydrocarbons in crude oil are mostly alkanes. Draw the displayed formulae of the first **four** alkanes and write down the name of each one next to its drawing.

    **(i)**                                      (2 marks)    **(ii)**                                      (2 marks)

    ................................................................    ................................................................

    **(iii)**                                   (2 marks)    **(iv)**                                    (2 marks)

    ................................................................    ................................................................

**(d)** Which one of the first four alkanes that you have drawn will have the highest boiling point? (1 mark)

**(e)** What makes alkanes relatively unreactive? (2 marks)

**(f)** Shorter-chain hydrocarbons are in greater demand as fuels. Why is this? (2 marks)

3. **(a)** Write down **one advantage** or **disadvantage** of using fossil fuels that affects people. (1 mark)

**(b)** Write down **one advantage** or **disadvantage** of using fossil fuels that affects the economy. (1 mark)

**(c)** Write down **one advantage** or **disadvantage** of using fossil fuels that affects the environment. (1 mark)

# AQA GCSE Science A Workbook Answers

## Keeping Healthy (pp 4–10)

1. Eating a diet high in animal fats — Heart attack
   Eating too much salt — High blood pressure
   Eating too many high energy foods — Obesity
   Drinking excessive alcohol — Liver disease
   (*1 correct = 1 mark; 2 correct = 2 marks; All 4 correct = 3 marks*)
2. Reduce his calorie intake; Increase the amount of exercise he does.
3. liver; inherited factors; saturated
4. **(a)** Antibiotics
   **(b)** Produce antibodies; Produce antitoxins.
   **(c)** To alleviate the symptoms of the flu.
5. **(a)**

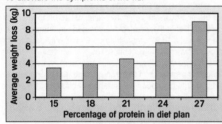

   **(b)** **Any two from:** Age group of people; All obese; Daily calorie intake; Similar foods
   **(c)** **Any two from:** Sex of group; How obese they were; Amount of exercise taken
   **(d)** The higher the amount of protein in a diet plan; the more weight is likely to be lost.
6. **(a)** Agar
   **(b)** To sterilise it/kill any microbes on it.
   **(c)** To prevent microbes from the air getting in; to prevent possible harmful organisms getting out.
   **(d)** 25°C
7. **(a)** It had arisen from a mutation; of an older strain of the virus.
   **(b)** A disease that has travelled between countries.
   **(c)** 1300
   **(d)** 8–10th May
   **(e)** People were not immune; There was no vaccine available.
   **(f)** They are found in cells; and treatment often damages the body's cells.
8. dead/weakened; antibodies; immune
9. **(a)** Mumps, measles, rubella
   **(b)** 84%
   **(c)** 2003–2004
   **(d)** **Accept one from:** Loss of public confidence about the safety of the vaccination; Reports about a possible link between the MMR vaccine and autism.
10. **(a)** malnourished
    **(b)** foods from each food group.
    **(c)** increase
11. **(a)** A jelly-like substance containing nutrients; that bacteria need to grow/A culture medium
    **(b)** To kill any microbes.
    **(c)** So the bacteria will grow.
    **(d)** **(i)** and **(ii)** See diagram below.

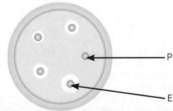

12. **(a)** Within the population of TB bacteria there may be a few organisms with natural resistance to isoniazid; This could be a result of a mutation; When a patient is treated with isoniazid, all the sensitive bacteria are killed; This allows resistant bacteria to quickly grow and multiply.
    **(b)** If a bacterium develops resistance to one of the antibiotics; it will still be killed by the second antibiotic.
    **(c)** Not overprescribe antibiotics; Not use antibiotics to treat minor infections.

## Nerves and Hormones (pp 11–18)

1. **(a)** Smell
   **(b)** Ears
   **(c–d)** **Any two from:** Touch; Temperature; Pain; Pressure

2. **(a)** To protect itself
   **(b–c)**

   **(d)** When the electrical impulse reaches the synapse, a chemical transmitter substance is released by the first neurone; The transmitter activates receptors on the second neurone; causing a new electrical impulse to be generated in the second neurone; The transmitter is then destroyed.
3. **(A)** brain
   **(B)** spinal nerves
   **(C)** spinal cord
4. **(a)** **(i)** C
       **(ii)** A
       **(iii)** B (*1 correct = 1 mark; All correct = 2 marks*)
   **(b)** motor neurone
5. glands; in the blood; progesterone; follicle-stimulating hormone
6. **(a)** **(i)** light
       **(ii)** eye
       **(iii)** eye
   **(b)** Reflex
7. **This is a model answer that would score full marks.** The shoot will always grow upwards against the direction of gravity and the roots will always grow downwards in the direction of gravity. This is called geotropism.
8. **(a)** It is cheaper; It reduces the need for repeated cycles of hormone therapy (injections).
   **(b)** It only has an 18% success rate; Some doctors worry about the safety of using eggs for the children born.
9. **(a)** **Any two from:** Amount of water; Amount of light; Temperature; Size of cuttings at start.
   **(b)** Bob's rooting compound makes the roots grow faster; so the plants themselves grow faster.
   **(c)** **Any of the following:** Willow tree twigs may be difficult to find; It takes a lot of time to make the compound; The compound might not keep for very long.
   **(d)** auxin
10. **(a)** ovaries
    **(b)** People taking oestrogen pills experienced unpleasant side-effects.
    **(c)** Oestrogen inhibits the production of FSH.
11. **(a)** Accept any answer between 10% and 15%
    **(b)** 8%
    **(c)** 4%; Kills nearly all weeds; Will be cheaper than 8%; Twice as much weedkiller will mean more damage to environment.
    **(d)** **Any two from:** Type of weeds in the land; Amount of weedkiller used, e.g. application rate; Aspect of land, e.g. shade/sun.
    **(e)** **(i)** They may get into the pond and harm aquatic life, e.g. water creatures.
        **(ii)** They may kill the hedge (which is a habitat for many organisms).
12. **(a)** stimulus, receptor, sensory neurone, relay neurone, motor neurone, effector, response
    (*All correct = 3 marks, 4 or more in correct order = 2 marks, stimulus at start and response at end = 1 mark*).
    **(b)** Between sensory neurone and relay neurone; Between relay neurone and motor neurone (*either answer correct*).
13. A; D; E; G
14. **(a)** In sweat; In urine
    **(b)** **One of the following:** Temperature; Blood glucose/sugar levels

## The Use and Abuse of Drugs (pp 19–21)

1. **(a)** Cannabis
   **(b)** Statins/aspirin
   **(c)** Alcohol/aspirin
2. anabolic steroids; banned; testosterone; heart/liver.
3. **(a)** nicotine; heroin
   **(b)** **Accept one from:** Drugs alter the body's chemistry; People get withdrawal symptoms.
4. **(a)** 1. New drug is made in the laboratory.
       2. Drug is tested in the laboratory using tissue culture.
       3. Trials using low doses of drug on a small number of healthy volunteers.

4. Clinical trials involving large numbers of patients and volunteers.
5. Drug is passed for use by general public.
   (*All 4 correct = 3 marks; 3 correct = 2 marks; 2 correct = 1 mark*)
- **(b)** To check for toxicity (they are not harmful); To check for efficacy (they work).
- **(c)** **(i)** A dummy drug
  - **(ii)** The group given the placebo will act as a control group; The effect of any drug can be compared against people not taking the drug.

5. **(a)** **Any two from:** Cannabis can be used to treat the symptoms of a number of diseases; Cannabis is not addictive; Smoking cannabis is less harmful than smoking cigarettes.
   - **(b)** **Any two from:** Cannabis use has been linked to mental illness; Cannabis may act as a 'gateway' drug to more addictive drugs such as heroin and cocaine; Cannabis smoke contains around 400 chemicals.
6. **Any two from:** This could be seen as encouraging people to eat high fat foods; High cholesterol is only one problem caused by high fat diets; A statin pill will not protect against other problems caused by a high fat diet, e.g. obesity; Statins need to be taken regularly to be effective; Statins can have side-effects.
7. **Any two from:** It had not been tested as treatment for morning sickness; It had not been tested on pregnant women; It could harm the unborn baby.
8. **(a)** Cholesterol builds up in arteries that take blood to heart muscle; Can cause narrowing of arteries/heart disease.
   - **(b)** Heart attack/chest pains/shortness of breath
   - **(c)** liver
9. **(a)** Far more people smoke than use illegal drugs.
   - **(b)** **One of the following:** Crime – people steal to get money to buy drugs; Family breakdown
   - **(c)** **One of the following:** People unable to work; People claiming benefits because they cannot work; Cost to justice system in dealing with crime.

## Interdependence and Adaptation (pp 22–28)

1. For catching seals – C
   For warmth – B
   To help grip the ice – D
   For camouflage – A
   (*1 correct = 1 mark; 2 correct = 2 marks; All 4 correct = 3 marks*)
2. **(a)** They present a large surface area for blood to flow through and lose heat.
   - **(b)** **One of the following:** Colour of fur; Thickness of fur; Amount of fat.
3. **(a)** Allow it to grip/stick to trees.
   - **(b)** Camouflage so it won't be seen.
   - **(c)** To catch insects/prey.
4. **(a)** Ben's
   - **(b)**

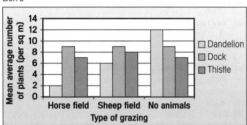

   - **(c)** Horse field
   - **(d)** 6 × 1000; = 6000
   - **(e)** Both horses and sheep eat dandelions; Horses eat more dandelions than sheep; Neither horses nor sheep graze on dock or thistles.
   - **(f)** **Any one from:** They could take more quadrats; They could repeat the experiment on a different piece of land; They could repeat investigation at different times of year
   - **(g)** **Any three from:** Light; Space; Water; Nutrients
5. **(a)** **(i-ii)** Very high temperatures; Very little water to drink
   - **(b)** **(i)** This stores water
     - **(ii)** This reduces the amount of water the cactus loses through its leaves
6. extremophiles
7. **Any three from:** Many tiny airborne seeds – seeds can be carried a long way and even if many die, plenty will grow into adult plants; Sharp, prickly leaves – this will deter animals from eating the thistle; Very deep tap root – allows plant to get more water/makes it difficult to pull up; Long flowering period – plenty of opportunity for insects to pollinate plants; Plant can grow in poor soil – it can grow where other plants might not be able to.
8. indicator; polluted; oxygen
9. **(a)** There was a slight rise in 1974; But since then the numbers have decreased rapidly between 1976 and 1986; And decreased slowly between 1986 and 2002 (*1 mark for dates*)
   - **(b)** Farmers have cut down hedgerows and/or trees so the birds have had nowhere to nest and their food source has been reduced.
   - **(c)** **Any of the following:** Plant more trees; Encourage farmers to plant hedgerows; Encourage farmers to leave field edges wild as food for birds; Use fewer pesticides
10. **Any two from:** Food; Mates; Territory
11. **(a)** **Any one from:** The direction of the wind; Transect A may have passed over more roads, which could have caused increased pollution/sulfur dioxide levels.

- **(b)** The industrial area was producing sulfur dioxide pollution.
- **(c)** The trees would have been different heights; This would affect the reliability of the data.
- **(d)** **Any one from:** Width of tree trunks; Distance of nearest tree to transect; Type of tree.

## Energy and Biomass in Food Chains (pp 29–31)

1. **(a)** Heron
   Frog
   Insect
   Marsh plants
   (*1 correct = 1 mark; 2 correct = 2 marks; All 4 correct = 3 marks*)
   - **(b)** the Sun
   - **(c)** Energy is lost at every stage (trophic level) of the food chain and therefore there is less energy available for growth.
   - **(d)** The number of frogs will decrease; Because they have less food.
2. **(a)** 10%
   - **(b)** 10%
   - **(c)** 10% of 10% = 0.1 × 0.1; = 0.01 = 1%
   - **(d)** All of the energy in the vegetable gets passed on to the human in a vegetarian diet; If the vegetable is eaten by an animal, when the animal is eaten by a human, the human will only get a tenth of the energy that was in the vegetable. The rest will have been used by the animal for growth, producing heat, movement and waste.
3. **Energy used for any three of following:** Movement of animals; Respiration by animals; Maintaining body temperature of birds; Lost via animal waste

## Waste Materials from Plants and Animals (pp 32–35)

1. Grass cuttings; Vegetable peelings; Teabags
2. algae; glucose; decomposers; decomposers
   (*1 correct = 1 mark; 2 correct = 2 marks; All 4 correct = 3 marks*)
3. **(a)** Jim
   - **(b)** Jim's compost will be warm (black plastic) and will get oxygen because it is turned over; These are good conditions for bacteria to grow and digest the waste.
   - **(c)** **Any two from:** If organic waste is sent to landfill, it will produce methane, which is a greenhouse gas; Recycling the waste means less space is taken up in landfill sites; People will not need to buy peat-based compost (destruction of peat bogs is an environmental issue).
   - **(d)** The compost can be used on plants, avoiding the need to buy compost or fertilisers.
4. **(a)** Feeding D; Excretion A; Photosynthesis B; Respiration C
   - **(b)** Combustion (burning)
5. **(a)** Tube D; Because it is warm and moist.
   - **(b)** The soil/air/surface of the leaf
   - **(c)** So that air could get in.
   - **(d)** **Accept one from:** They could count the number of whole discs left at the end; They could record what fraction/percentage of leaf discs decayed and find an average. They could measure percentage decrease in mass of discs by measuring mass before and after time in soil.

## Genetic Variation and its Control (pp 36–40)

1. **(a)** A – nucleus; B – cytoplasm; C – chromosomes; D – cell membrane.
   - **(b)** fusion; DNA; variation
2. A; B; F
3. **(a)** B  **(b)** E  **(c)** B  **(d)** I
4. **(a)** Enzymes
   - **(b)** **Any two from:** They reproduce rapidly; They can be grown in large vats; They produce large quantities of insulin.
5. **(a)** characteristics; sexual; specialised; implanted; wombs
   - **(b)** The original sheep may only have one or two young; By using embryo transplants, many new sheep can be produced in the same time period.
   - **(c)** They all came from cells from the same embryo; So will have the same genes as each other; They will have a mixture of genes; Inherited from mother and father.
   - **(d)** To treat diseases.
6. **(a)** **Any three from:** GM crops give higher yields; GM crops are insect resistant, reducing the use of pesticide; GM crops take up less land, leaving more for wildlife; GM crops can be enriched with nutrients, so are more healthy.
   - **(b)** GM crops might breed with wild plants; GM crops may harm the insects that feed on them.
   - **(c)** **Any one from:** To extend shelf life; Drought resistance
7. **(a)** 1 – A body cell is taken from a prize bull.
     2 – An unfertilised egg cell is taken from cow B.
     3 – The nucleus is removed from the egg cell.
     4 – The egg cell is fused with the body cell.
     5 – The fused cells start to divide to form an embryo.
     6 – The embryo is implanted into the womb of another cow.
     (*All correct = 3 marks; 3 correct = 2 marks; 2 correct = 1 mark*)
   - **(b)** They are given an electric shock.

8. (a) one
   (b) gametes
   (c) the same as
   (d) clone

## Evolution (pp 41–45)

1. (a) The giraffes would have been born with long neck or short neck genes; They could not grow long necks and change their genes during their lifetime.
   (b) **Any two from:** It was against their religion (God created the Earth); There was insufficient evidence at the time; People did not know about genes and mechanisms of inheritance.
   (c) five million
2. (a) 210 million years ago
   (b) Cretaceous
   (c) They have discovered fossils.
   (d) Lizard
   (e) Archosaur
3. All species in existence have developed from simple life forms over a period of approximately 3 billion years.
4. **This is a model answer that would score full marks.** Darwin's theory is that there is much variation within species and that species compete for food, mates, etc. The individuals within the species that are the best suited/adapted will be more successful and will survive. They will therefore breed and pass on their genes to their offspring. This is known as 'survival of the fittest'. Those individuals that are not well adapted are less likely to survive and may become extinct.
5. (a) Some babies' skulls were found in their mothers' pouches.
   (b) It had giant claws.
   (c) The fossil finds suggest that they travelled in herds.
   (d) Extinct
6. (a) There are more striped snails in the countryside because the stripes camouflage them; In the forest, there are more plain snails where they blend in with the forest floor.
   (b) Brown; Because it is dark in the forest and the brown blends in with trees and forest floor.
   (c) Scotland
   (d) Less brown-shelled snails – brown shells may cause them to overheat; More yellow-shelled snails – no need to warm up the snail.

## The Fundamental Ideas in Chemistry (pp 46–50)

1. (a) Electron
   (b) Proton/neutron
   (c) Neutron/proton
   (d) Nucleus
2. (a) A substance that is made entirely from one type of atom; There are over 100 elements.
   (b) In the Periodic Table; In periods/groups
   (c) Fluorine (F); Silicon (Si); Tungsten (W).
3. (a) A substance composed of two or more different elements; chemically bonded together.
   (b) Ionic; Covalent.
4. (a) The proportion of the atoms; of each element making up the compound.
   (b) (i)  $2H_2O = (4 \times H) + (2 \times O)$
       (ii)  $2NaOH = (2 \times Na) + (2 \times O) + (2 \times H)$
       (iii)  $Mg(OH)_2 = (1 \times Mg) + (2 \times O) + (2 \times H)$
   (c) (i)  2
       (ii)  $2(2 \times Al) = 4Al$, $2(3 \times O) = 60$
       (iii)  1
       (iv)  $(1 \times H)$, $(1 \times N)$, $(3 \times O)$
       (v)  3
       (vi)  $3(2 \times Fe) = 6Fe$, $3(3 \times O) = 90$
5. (a) (i)  Reactants – compounds or elements that react together.
       (ii)  Products – made by the reactants during the reaction.
   (b) sodium and chlorine (reactants); sodium chloride (product).
6. The number of atoms of each type; must be the same on both sides of the equation.
7. (a) magnesium; oxygen; magnesium oxide.
   (b) 2Mg and 2MgO are needed; so the same number of circles of Mg and O are on both sides.
8. (a)

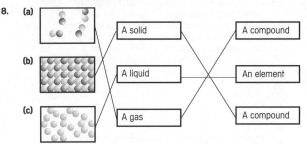

   (b)
   (c)

9. (a) <u>hydrogen</u> + <u>oxygen</u> ⟶ (water)

   $\underline{2H_2} + \underline{O_2}$ ⟶ $(2H_2O)$

   (b) <u>aluminium</u> + <u>iron oxide</u> ⟶ (iron) + (aluminium oxide)

   $\underline{Fe_2O_3} + \underline{2Al}$ ⟶ $(Al_2O_3)$ + $(2Fe)$

   (c) <u>octane</u> + <u>oxygen</u> ⟶ (carbon dioxide) + (water)

   $\underline{2C_8H_{18}} + \underline{25O_2}$ ⟶ $(16CO_2)$ + $(18H_2O)$

   (d) <u>sodium</u> + <u>water</u> ⟶ (sodium hydroxide) + (hydrogen)

   $\underline{2Na} + \underline{2H_2O}$ ⟶ $(2NaOH)$ + $(H_2)$

   (e) <u>sodium hydroxide</u> + <u>hydrochloric acid</u> ⟶
   (sodium chloride) + (water)

   $\underline{HCl} + \underline{NaOH}$ ⟶ $(NaCl)$ + $(H_2O)$

   (f) <u>hydrogen peroxide</u> ⟶ (water) + (oxygen)

   $\underline{2H_2O_2}$ ⟶ $(O_2)$ + $(2H_2O)$

10. True – (a); (b); (e); (g); (i); (m); (n).
    False – (c); (d); (f); (h); (i); (j); (k); (o).
11. (a) Calcium (b) Hydrogen (c) Potassium (d) Magnesium (e) Sulfur

## Limestone and Building Materials (pp 51–55)

1. (a) cement; glass
   (b) Calcium carbonate
2. (a) calcium oxide
   (b) calcium oxide + water ⟶ calcium hydroxide.
   (c) It is a chemical reaction in which an acid and a base react with a formation of a salt and water to give a solution with a pH of 7.
3. (a) Glass is made by heating; a mixture of limestone, sand and soda (sodium carbonate).
   (b) Cement is produced by roasting powdered limestone with powdered clay in a rotary kiln.
   (c) **(i–iii) In any order:** Water; Sand; Gravel
4. brick – baked clay; glass – melted sand; wood – trees; steel – iron; iron – iron ore; cement – limestone and clay. (*All 6 correct = 4 marks; 4–5 correct = 3 marks; 2–3 correct = 2 marks; 1 correct = 1 mark.*)
5. (a) Construction and architecture.
   (b) Powdered limestone is extracted from quarries or mines and usually requires mechanical crushing. The fineness of the limestone is important in determining how quickly it reacts with soil acidity.
   (c) Making glass.
   (d) Making cement, mortar and concrete.
   (e) Cement is produced by roasting a mixture of powdered limestone with powdered clay in a rotary kiln. When cement is mixed with water, sand and crushed rock, a slow chemical reaction produces a hard, stone-like building material called concrete.
6. (a) **Any two from:** Limestone is a valuable natural resource, used to make things such as glass and concrete that are used in everyday life; Limestone quarrying provides employment opportunities that support the local economy in towns around the quarry; Quarries can be used as lakes and other recreational areas afterwards.
   (b) **Any two from:** Quarrying is a heavy industry that creates dust; Noise; Heavy traffic.
   (c) **Any relevant points including:** Environmental problems are caused by quarrying limestone; Dust pollution; Damaged landscape; Buildings on the site take up room; Noise from explosives; More lorries on country lanes; After use, the quarry has to be landscaped.
7. (a) (i)  Can be cut into blocks easily
       (ii)  Can be eroded by acid rain
       (iii)  Strong under compression
       (iv)  Weak under tension
       (v)  Transparent
       (vi)  Fragile
   (b) Wood is less versatile; and inappropriate for uses where these materials are used.
8. (a) Combines hardness of concrete; with strength of steel
   (b) iron – haematite ore; brick – baked clay; glass – sand

## Metals and their Uses (pp 56–58)

1. A rock that contains minerals with important elements, including the oxides of metals, and is economically worth extracting.
2. (a) **Accept any suitable answer, e.g.:** Metals such as copper, silver, gold and platinum are unreactive and can be extracted by various chemical reactions. Gold, because it is so unreactive, is found as the native metal and not as a compound, so it does not need to be chemically separated.
   (b) Many metals can be extracted from their metal oxide ore by heating with carbon, e.g. copper can be obtained by heating copper oxide with carbon or electrolysis of $Al_2O_3$ etc.
   (c) Reduction.
   (d) By heating with carbon.

3.  (a) Mostly iron and some carbon, although it can contain more than five elements.
    (b) By adding different amounts of carbon and other metals.
    (c) Steel.
4.  (a) A mixture of two or more elements of which at least one is a metal.
    (b) Because it is more difficult for the atoms; to slide past each other.
5.  brass helps kill some bacteria – hospital door handles; normal steel is strong and cheap – general construction; solder has a low melting point – sticking metals together; stainless steel is strong and will not rust – knives and forks; bronze is easy to cast into shapes – statues.
    (All 5 correct = 3 marks; 3–4 correct = 2 marks; 1–2 correct = 1 mark)
6.  Carbon is removed from iron by blowing oxygen into the molten metal; It reacts with the carbon producing carbon monoxide and carbon dioxide, which escape from the molten metal; Enough oxygen is used to achieve steel with the desired carbon content. (Other metals are often added, such as vanadium and chromium.)
7.  (a) High carbon steel
    (b) Easily shaped
    (c) Stainless steel
    (d) Cutlery and sinks
8.  Although aluminium and titanium are two metals with a low density, titanium is twice as strong as aluminium; but only 60% more dense; so it is more suitable for making hip replacement joints.
9.  (a) (i–iii): **Any three from:** Scandium; Titanium; Vanadium; Chromium; Manganese; Iron; Cobalt; Nickel; Copper; Zinc; Yttrium; Zirconium; Niobium; Molybdenum; Technetium; Ruthenium; Rhodium; Palladium; Silver; Cadmium; Hafnium; Tantalum; Tungsten; Rhenium; Osmium; Iridium; Platinum; Gold; Mercury; Rutherfordium; Dubnium; Seaborgium; Bohrium; Hassium; Meitnerium; Ununnilium; Unununium; Ununbium.
    (b) (i–iii): **Any three from:** They are good conductors of heat and electricity; They can be hammered or bent into shape easily; They are less reactive than alkali metals such as sodium; They have higher melting points (but mercury is a liquid at room temperature); They are hard and tough.
10. (a) Electrolysis
    (b) (i–iii) **In any order:** Saves resources; Saves energy; Reduces costs.
11. Smart alloys have unusual properties. e.g. nitinol is known as a shape memory alloy; If it is bent out of shape, it returns to its original shape when it is either heated or an electric current is passed through it.

## Crude Oil and Fuels (pp 59–62)

1.  (a) A compound that contains the elements carbon and hydrogen only.
    (b) Fractional distillation.
    (c) Because they have different boiling points, the substances in crude oil can be separated using fractional distillation; Smaller molecules have lower boiling points because there are weaker intermolecular forces between them.
2.  (a) C = carbon, H = hydrogen.
    (b) Covalent bonds.
    (c) (i) Methane;      (ii) Ethane;
    (iii) Propane;
    (iv) Butane;
    (d) Butane.
    (e) They are saturated compounds; they have no double bonds.
    (f) **Any two from:** Hydrocarbons with small molecules make better fuels than hydrocarbons with large molecules because they are volatile; Flow easily; Are easily ignited.
3.  (a) **Accept any suitable answer, e.g.:** Fossil fuels are readily available and they are suitable for many applications (advantage).
    (b) **Accept any suitable answer, e.g.:** Relatively inexpensive (advantage).
    (c) **Accept any suitable answer, e.g.:** They can cause pollution and will eventually be used up (disadvantage).
4.  (a) (i) Renewable and can be used to power vehicles.
        (ii) Some people are concerned about whether it is ethical to use food crops in this way, instead of using them to feed hungry people.
        (iii) A clean fuel. It produces water.
        (iv) Some hydrogen-powered vehicles have already been made and are on the road, but there are few of them because there are difficulties in making and handling hydrogen.
    (b) **This is a model answer that would score full marks.** The majority of hydrogen used is made by reacting steam with coal or natural gas, both of which are non-renewable resources. Hydrogen can also be made by passing electricity through water. However, the disadvantage of this method is that most electricity is generated using coal and other fossil fuels so that any pollution from burning these fuels just happens at the power station instead of from burning petrol and diesel in the vehicle itself.

5.  It may have to be pumped to the surface.
6.  **Accept any suitable answer, e.g.:** Land has to be cleared, destroying habitats; Oil slicks if spilled.
7.  **Any one from:** Pumping oil from under the sea using oil rigs is dangerous; It has to be transported from the oil rig using pipes or tankers; If a tanker runs aground oil can spill, forming an oil slick that can cause harm to wildlife and habitats.
8.  (a) (i) Ethanol can be made by a process called fermentation; This converts sugar from sugar cane or sugar beet into ethanol and carbon dioxide. Single-celled fungi, called yeast, contain enzymes that are natural catalysts for making this process happen.
        (ii) Ethanol can be manufactured by reacting ethene (from cracking crude oil fractions) with steam; A catalyst of phosphoric acid is used to ensure a fast reaction.
    (b) (i) **Any two from:** Sugar from plant material; Little energy required; Warm; Normal pressure.
        (ii) **Any one from:** Impure – needs treatment; A lot of workers needed; Rate of reaction slow; Batch process (stop-start).
    (c) (i) **Any two from:** Ethene and steam; Continuous process (runs all the time); Labour – few workers needed; Product pure.
        (ii) **Any one from:** High temperature and pressure conditions needed; A lot of energy needed.

## Other Useful Substances from Crude Oil (pp 63–67)

1.  (a)
    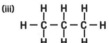
    (b) a = 8; b = 18        (c) Alkene
    (d) A – Liquid alkane on mineral fibre
        B – Aluminium oxide
        C – Ethene
        D – Gentle or occasional heat
        E – Very strong heat
        F – Water
        (All correct = 4 marks; 4–5 correct = 3 marks; 2–3 correct = 2 marks; 1 correct = 1 mark)
2.  (a) methane
    (b) A compound that contains at least one carbon to carbon double bond.
    (c) (i) Propene        (ii) $C_3H_8$
        (iii)                 (iv)

3.  **Any two from:** When ethanol is made through fermentation, it is found in alcoholic drinks such as wine and beer; It is also useful as a fuel for use in cars and other vehicles when it is usually mixed with petrol; Ethanol manufactured from crude oil is used as a raw material for other chemicals.
4.  (a) They have a carbon to carbon double bond.
    (b) The reactive double bonds; open up; and join to other alkene molecules.
    (c) The double bond in each ethene molecule must be broken.
5.  
6.  (a)                      (b) poly(chloroethene).
7.  (a) large; chains; plastic; polymerisation.
    (b) ethene – poly(ethene); propene – poly(propene); styrene – poly(styrene); chloroethene – poly (vinyl chloride).
    (c) They have different groups; attached to the carbon atoms in the polymer chain.
    (d) They will cause disposal problems.
    (e) Recycle.
8.  High pressure; A catalyst.
9.  (a) A long chain of carbon atoms joined together with a repeating pattern of monomer units.
    (b) Because the polymer chains have time to move past each other easily when it is poured like a liquid but they become tangled up when moved too quickly and behave like a solid.
    (c) Use more/less concentrated sodium tetraborate solution.
10. (a) Polystyrene
    (b) Polyester, nylon
    (c) Polythene
    (d) Polystyrene
    (e) Polyester, nylon
    (f) Keeps the wearer dry from rain
    (g) Allows water vapour to escape, keeping the wearer dry from condensed sweat

## Plant Oils and their Uses (pp 68–71)

1.  (a)  Crushed and pressed; Dissolved in a solvent.
    (b)  Rapeseed oil; Cooking oil.
    (c)  They can provide a lot of energy.
    (d)  **Any three from:** Carbon neutral; Renewable; Biodegradable; Less toxic; Preserves crude oil.
    (e)  It is incompatible; It costs more to make; There is a limited supply.
2.  (a)  (i)  bromine water
        (ii)  emulsion.
    (b)  (i)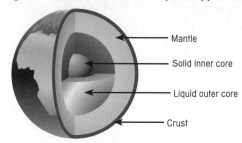
        (ii)  Bromine atoms attach to the carbon atoms.
3.  (a)  The forces between the molecules in oil and water are different.
    (b)  To form an emulsion to prevent the oil and vinegar from separating.
4.  (a)  saturated; fish oil (*both correct = 1 mark*)
    (b)  liquid
    (c)  butter; no (*both correct = 1 mark*)
    (d)  olive oil; more than one (*both correct = 1 mark*)
5.  (a)  They provide energy.
    (b)  **Any one from:** Obesity; Heart disease; High blood pressure.
6.  (a)  Oils are converted into a solid fat by reacting them with hydrogen gas at about 60°C; with a nickel catalyst.
    (b)  ethene + hydrogen ⟶ ethane
7.  (a)  **Any two from:** To improve: Flavour; Texture; Longevity; Appearance.
    (b)  Allergic reactions; Masks taste
8.  Hydrogenation.

## Changes in the Earth and its Atmosphere (pp 72–77)

1.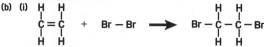

    Mantle

    Solid inner core

    Liquid outer core

    Crust

2.  Plate tectonics explained why earthquakes and volcanoes were concentrated in specific places; around the boundaries of moving plates; The match in shape between the east coast of South America and the west coast of Africa suggests both were once part of a single continent; There are similar patterns of rocks and similar fossils on both sides of the Atlantic, including the fossil remains of land animals who would have been unable to swim across an ocean.
3.  (a)  Alfred Wegener proposed that the Earth's continents were once joined together, but gradually moved apart over millions of years; The continents of Africa and South America look as though they were once joined together; Wegener's theory offered an explanation of the existence of similar fossils and rocks on continents that are far apart from each other.
    (b)  It was difficult to work out what the mechanism was that could make whole continents move.
4.  Earthquakes and volcanoes.
5.  Only a short warning time; The process of plate tectonics is very complex.
6.  If the plates are moving sideways, stresses build up at the plate boundary; When the stress reaches some critical value, the plates slip suddenly, causing an earthquake.
7.  (a)  A constructive plate margin occurs when the plates are moving apart, as at mid-ocean ridges; Volcanoes are produced as molten magma is allowed to escape. This happens in Iceland, for example.
    (b)  A destructive plate margin occurs when the plates are moving towards each other; The edges of the plates crumple, and one plate 'dives' under the other. This is also known as subduction. It produces mountains, like the Andes.
    (c)  A – Constructive plate margin; B – Destructive plate margin.
8.  (a)  Alfred Wegener.
    (b)  Alfred Wegener proposed the theory of continental drift at the beginning of the 20th century. His idea was that the Earth's continents were once joined together; but gradually moved apart over millions of years.
    (c)  Convection currents in the mantle; result in the plates moving.
9.  (a)  At plate boundaries.
    (b)  They are less dense.
    (c)  It cools very quickly so the crystals do not have a long time to form.
10. (a)  (i–ii)  Use of fossil fuels; Deforestation.
    (b)  It is inert; It is unreactive.

11. (a)  (i)  Burning fossil fuels.
        (ii)  Carbon dioxide builds up as more is being produced and less consumed by trees removed during deforestation.
        (iii)  From natural and man-made fires (such as forest and bushfires, burning of crop residues, and sugarcane fire-cleaning). The burning of fossil fuels also contributes to carbon monoxide production.
    (b)  **Answer may mention the following:** Humans using fossil fuels; Releases carbon dioxide and sulfur dioxide into the atmosphere; Global warming and acid rain can result.
        (*Maximum 2 marks*)
    (c)  **Any three from:** Use less fossil fuels; Switch to carbon neutral fuels; More efficient cars etc; Remove pollutants at source, e.g. sulfur scrubbers.
12. (a)  (i)  Nitrogen    (ii)  Oxygen
        (iii)  Others such as carbon dioxide.
    (b)  (i)  2    (ii)  4
        (iii)  3    (iv)  6
        (v)  5    (vi)  7
        (vii)  1
        (*All 7 correct = 4 marks; 5–6 correct = 3 marks; 3–4 correct = 2 marks; 1–2 correct = 1 mark*)
13. (a)

| Name of process | Gas made | Gas used up |
|---|---|---|
| 1 combustion | carbon dioxide | oxygen |
| 2 respiration (sheep) | carbon dioxide | oxygen |
| 3 respiration (plant) | carbon dioxide | oxygen |
| 4 photosynthesis | oxygen | carbon dioxide |

    (b)  A lot more carbon dioxide is used up during photosynthesis than is given out during respiration and combustion.
    (c)  Plants need carbon dioxide to photosynthesize; Photosynthesis produces the oxygen that animals need to respire.
    (d)  There is a balance between the processes that use up carbon dioxide and make oxygen and the processes that use up oxygen and make carbon dioxide.
    (e)  It is very unreactive.

## Energy Transfer (pp 78–81)

1.  Heat energy from the Sun reaches the houses by thermal radiation – White is a poor absorber of thermal radiation.
2.  (a)  Cup D; It has a small surface area; and is white so does not emit heat well.
    (b)  Cup A; It has a large surface area; and is black so emits heat well.
3.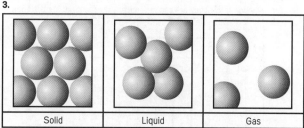

    | Solid | Liquid | Gas |

4.  **This is a model answer that would score full marks:** In a solid, the particles vibrate around a fixed point. As the solid is heated, the particles gain energy and move faster. When they have enough energy, the particles can move around. The solid 'melts' and becomes liquid.
5.  **This is a model answer that would score full marks:** In a liquid, the particles can move around but are very close to one another. As the liquid is heated, the particles gain energy and move faster. When they have enough energy, they are able to move away from each other. The liquid 'boils' and evaporates to become a gas.
6.  (a)

    hot air          cold air

    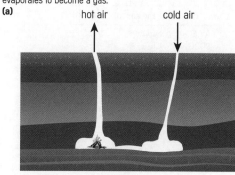

    (b)  Convection

(c) **Any five from:** As the air is heated, particles move faster (*This point is essential for full marks*); The air expands; The air becomes less dense; The hot, less dense air rises; The cold, denser air sinks; Creates a convection current.

7. The cold air is more dense than warm air; so sinks to the bottom of the freezer.

8. (a) Particles are heated and vibrate more; This vibration is passed onto the next particle which then vibrates more and passes the energy along to the next and so on.
   (b) Free (de-localised) electrons

9. Air is a bad conductor; The meringue and sponge contain air bubbles; The white meringue is a bad absorber of thermal radiation; No fluid so no convection possible.

## Energy and Efficiency (pp 82–86)

1. (a) Warm; Dry
   (b) 3 years
   (c) **Any one from:** Concern for the environment; Global warming; Reducing carbon footprint.

2. For particles to evaporate, they need enough energy to escape from the liquid. They get this energy from the surrounding particles. As water on the tongue evaporates; it takes energy from the blood flowing through the tongue; This helps to keep the dog cool.

3. (a)

| Method | Payback time |
|---|---|
| Double glazing | **(i)** 20 years |
| Loft insulation | **(ii)** 2 years |
| Cavity wall insulation | **(iii)** 10 years |
| Draft proofing | **(iv)** 3 years |

   (b) Loft insulation

4. (a) **Any one from:** It does not make a difference; There is no correlation.
   (b) The reflective glass is more efficient; Its U-value is lower in every case.
   (c) **Any one from:** Cost; Appearance; Security.

5. (a) Black is a good absorber of thermal radiation.
   (b) To heat the water when it has not been sunny enough, or at night-time.
   (c) $E = m \times c \times \theta$;
   Energy needed = $100 \times 4200 \times 50 = 21\,000\,000$J;
   Energy per 1m² panel = 5 250 000J;
   Panel size needed = $\dfrac{21\,000\,000}{5\,250\,000} = 4$;
   Answer = 4m².

6. (a) Energy in the form of heat.
   (b) **Any one from:** They are cost-effective; They recharge the batteries.
   (c)

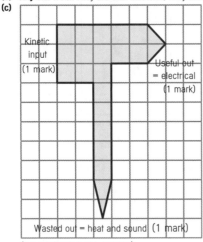

   (*1 mark for drawing diagram*)

7. (a) Hybrid: $\dfrac{9000}{10} = 900$ litres;
   Petrol: $\dfrac{9000}{6} = 1500$ litres;
   $1500 - 900 = 600$ litres;
   Hybrid saves $1500 - 900 = 600$ litres
   (b) $600 \times 1.25$; = £750
   (c) $\dfrac{3000}{750}$; = 4 years

## The Usefulness of Electrical Appliances (pp 87–94)

1.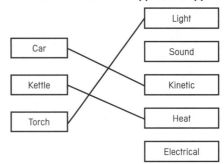

2. (a) (i) Electrical;   (ii) Kinetic
   (b) $500 \times 0.6$; = 300W
   (c) Total waste power output = total − useful;
   = 500 − 300 = 200W;
   $\dfrac{200}{2}$ = 100W sound = 100J (per second)
   (d) It disappears.

3. (a) 40% or 0.4
   (b)

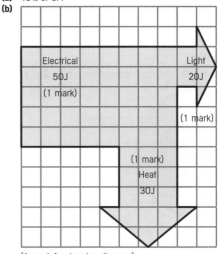

   (*1 mark for drawing diagram*)
   (c) 10% or 0.1
   (d) 180J of heat energy (*1 mark for number, 1 mark for unit*)
   (e) Yes; because it has a payback of just 6 months – you would get back the investment in only 6 months.

4. (a) (i) Chemical energy   (ii) Kinetic energy
   (iii) Sound energy   (iv) Thermal energy
   (b) 900J (*1 mark for number, 1 mark for unit*)
   (c) $\dfrac{900}{3000}$; = 30% or 0.3

5. (a) Chemical   (b) Gravitational potential
   (c) Gravitational potential   (d) Kinetic
   (e) Elastic/strain   (f) Kinetic
   (g) Chemical   (h) Light
   (*All correct = 5 marks, 6–7 correct = 4 marks, 4–5 correct = 3 marks, 2–3 correct = 2 marks, 1 correct = 1 mark*)

6. (a) electrical; heat; kinetic
   (b) $E = P \times t$;
   = $1200 \times 3 \times 60$;
   = 216 000J
   (c) $216\,000 \times 0.1$;
   = 21 600J

7. (a) Sound   (b) Heat
   (c) Electrical   (d) Light
   (e) Heat   (f) Light
   (*All correct = 4 marks, 4–5 correct = 3 marks, 2–3 correct = 2 marks, 1 correct = 1 mark*)

8. (a) Kilowatt hour (kWh)
   (b) $E = P \times t$;
   Energy = $0.5 \times 3 \times 7$;
   = 10.5kWh

9. (a) **Any two from:** Because they are inefficient; They waste a lot of energy; Leads to more pollution and a waste of resources.
   (b) (i) LED
   (ii) A − £180.00; B − £36.00; C − £6.00
   (iii) LED
   (iv) High initial cost.

10. **(a)** A – 258kWh; B – £18.06; C – 471kWh; D – £42.39; E – £60.45
    **(b)** **(i)** An independent website
    **(ii)** The salesman, television advert, or existing provider could be biased because they want you as a customer; the independent website should not be biased.
11. **(a)** Kinetic
    **(b)** **Any one from:** It spreads out; It is dissipated to the surroundings
    **(c)** 0.25 × 400 = 100W waste;
    E = P × t; = 100 × 120; = 12 000 Joules (J)
12. **(a)** Fridge
    **(b)** 0.25 × 24; = 6 kWh
    **(c)** 2 × 1 = 2; 0.25 × 24 = 6;
    0.5 × 6 = 3; 5 × 1 = 5;
    2 + 6 + 3 + 5 = 16 kWh;
    16 × 8 = 128p

## Methods We Use to Generate Electricity (pp 95–104)

1. **(a)** They have a long start-up time; Waste materials remain dangerous for a very long time.
   **(b)** Uranium; Plutonium
   **(c)** Nuclear fission
   **(d)** Both heat water to make steam; Steam turns a turbine; Turbine turns a generator.
   **(e)** Sulfur dioxide; Produces acid rain, which can kill plants; Carbon dioxide; Is a greenhouse gas and contributes to global warming.
2. **(a)** Renewable energy resources can be replaced; Non-renewable energy resources have a finite supply.
   **(b)** Nuclear
   **(c)** **(i)** **Any three from:** Cheaper to install; Quicker to install; Do not need to dig up the ground/roads to install; Easier to repair; Can transmit electricity at very high voltage, meaning more efficient electricity transmission.
   **(ii)** **Any two from:** Visual pollution; More likely to be damaged by weather; More dangerous (kite flyers etc.).
   **(d)** **Any two from:** Sometimes it is not windy, so need a backup supply; Wind energy is not suitable for meeting peaks in demand; We can't make the wind blow stronger when more energy is needed.
3. **(a)** Because fossil fuel power stations produce carbon dioxide, which is a greenhouse gas.
   **(b)** **Either:** Pumping carbon dioxide into the gas field displaces the methane; which then travels up the tube. **Or:** Pumping carbon dioxide into the oil field puts the oil under pressure; forcing it up to the oil rig.
   **(c)** A short start-up time means that it can be used to meet peak demand; when we know the demand is due to increase; e.g. at meal times when people switch on their ovens.
   **(d)** They do not produce sulfur dioxide.
4. Nuclear – Heats water to create steam that drives turbines; Solar cells – Produces electricity directly by converting energy from sunlight; Wind – Drives turbines directly; Biofuels – Heats water to create steam that drives turbines; Hydroelectric dam – Drives turbines directly.
5. **(a)** Black surfaces are good absorbers of thermal radiation; Shiny surfaces are good reflectors of thermal radiation.
   **(b)** **(i)** Because there are no fuel costs – sunlight is free.
   **(ii)** Because it costs money to build and maintain the station.
   **(c)** **Any two from:** Production of raw materials for building it; Loss of habitat; It takes up a large area of land.
   **(d)** The UK does not get enough sunlight to make it cost-effective.
6. **(a)** kinetic; turbine; generator; electricity
   **(b)** 1.5 × 24; = 36kWh
   **(c)** Savings per day = 36 × 10p; = 360p = £3.60;
   Payback = $\frac{\text{cost of turbine}}{\text{saving per day}}$ = $\frac{1800}{3.6}$ ; = 500 days
   **(d)** It's not always windy; Maintenance costs
   **(e)** **Any two from:** People want to be protected against electricity price rises; People want to help reduce pollution; Some places are too remote to be connected to the National Grid.
7. **(a)** Gravitational potential energy
   **(b)** They take very little time to increase productivity: Opening the valves to start the water flowing is almost instant.
   **(c)** The surplus electricity is used to pump the water in the lower reservoir up to the top reservoir; storing this energy for later use.
   **(d)** **Any two from:** No fuel costs; No atmospheric pollution; Renewable; Low electricity costs.
   **(e)** **Any four from:** Loss of animal habitat; Loss of farmland; Many towns and villages were flooded; Changes to the local ecosystem; The building process caused environmental damage; Very expensive.
8. **(a)** Geothermal energy
   **(b)** Hot rocks; and magma inside the Earth's crust.
9. **(a)** A – Step-up transformer; B – Step-down transformer
   **(b)** **Any two from:** It reduces the current; so the cables transfer less heat when the electricity is transmitted; so energy losses are reduced.
   **(c)** **Any two from:** It reduces the voltage; so it is safer to use; It increases the current.

10. **Any three from:** Reduces waste energy; Saves money/Means the bills are lower; Reduces environmental pollution; Preserves fuel reserves; Only a limited supply of electricity available
11. **(a)** Renewable energy sources can be used to drive turbines directly without burning anything.
    **(b)** **Accept any three or any other suitable answers:** Wind; Solar; Tidal; Geothermal
    **(c)** **Any two from:** Solar power can only produce small amounts of electricity; It is dependent upon light intensity; There is a high cost per unit.
    **(d)** **This is a model answer that would score full marks.** Producing electricity from a wind power station requires no fuel and little maintenance. Once set up, free energy is produced whenever the wind is blowing. However, wind power stations only produce small amounts of energy. It depends on the strength of the wind. A high capital outlay is required to build the power station and it is not very flexible in meeting demand.
    Hydroelectric power stations, on the other hand, produce large amounts of energy and they are flexible to meet demands. However, they take a long time to build, location is limited, they are expensive to build, and they rely on adequate rainfall.
    **(e)** There is a daily variation of tides and the waves affect output.
    **(f)** **Any two from:** No waste gases (apart from biomass); Low maintenance; Replaced faster than it is used.

## The Use of Waves (pp 105–116)

1. **(a)** A transverse wave
   **(b)** The number of waves per second.
   **(c)** By moving the hand up and down faster.
2. **(a)** A longitudinal wave
   **(b)** A sound wave
   **(c)** It is a point where the medium the wave is travelling in becomes less dense (the particles are further apart).
   **(d)** Energy
3. **(a)** **(i)** X-rays
   **(ii)** Ultraviolet
   **(iii)** Microwaves
   **(iv)** Radio waves

   **(b)** Reflection – Light bouncing off a mirror, enabling a car driver to see behind them; Refraction – Light changing direction leaving a swimming pool, making the pool look shallower; Diffraction – Light bouncing off a compact disc, splitting into many different colours.
   **(c)** Microwave
   **(d)** An opinion
   **(e)** **(i)** A
   **(ii)** **Any three from:** The study involved a large number of adults; The study lasted 10 years, so is short to medium term; Other dangers were not studied, so cannot say completely safe; Children were not included, so cannot make a conclusion about mobile phones; The study found no link between use and danger so cannot say it is not safe; No correlation between use and brain tumours, so can say it does not cause brain tumours. (*The fourth mark will be awarded for good English*)

4.

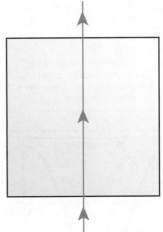

(*1 mark for the ray, 1 mark for direction arrows*)

**5.**

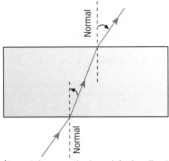

*(1 mark for normals, 1 mark for bending towards normal when entering, 1 mark for bending away from normal when leaving, 1 mark for arrows)*

**6.**

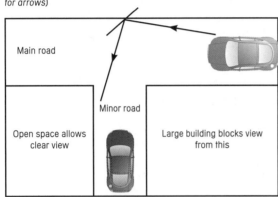

*(1 mark for rays, 1 mark for mirror in correct place, 1 mark for arrows pointing correct way and 1 mark for angle of incidence equal to angle of reflection.)*

**7. (a)**

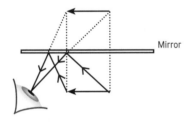

*(1 mark for each ray, 1 mark for arrows, 1 mark for image in correct place.)*

**(b)** Virtual; Upright

**8.** Radio waves – Television broadcasts; Microwaves – Satellite television; Infrared – Remote controls; Visible light – Photography

**9. (a)** Velocity = frequency × wavelength;

$$\text{wavelength} = \frac{\text{velocity}}{\text{frequency}}$$

$$= \frac{300\,000\,000}{100\,000\,000}; = 3m$$

**(b)** Diffraction occurs best when the gap size is similar to the wavelength; FM waves have a short wavelength so do not diffract much and do not bend round hills; Some radio waves have a much longer wavelength (1km), so diffract much more.

**10. (a)**

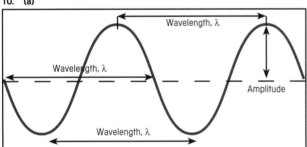

**(b)** Two

**(c)** Four

**(d)** $v = f \times \lambda$;

$= 20 \times 0.4; = 8m/s$

**11. (a)** There is one wave cycle every two seconds.

**(b)** $\text{Speed} = \dfrac{\text{distance}}{\text{time}}$

$= \dfrac{50}{10}; = 5m/s$

**(c)** $v = f \times \lambda$;

$\text{wavelength} = \dfrac{\text{speed}}{\text{frequency}}$;

$= \dfrac{5}{0.5}; = 10m$

**(d)** Five

**(e)** Refraction

**(f)** Diffraction

**12. (a)** Vibrations

**(b)** Longitudinal

**(c)** 3Hz

**(d)** Same frequency/wavelength; Bigger amplitude

**(e)** Same amplitude; More waves visible (short wavelength)

**(f)** It is unfair to youths who want to go shopping without causing trouble.

**(g)** Echo

**13. (a)** The Doppler effect.

**(b) This is a model answer.**
As the car moves away, the waves are stretched. This gives them a longer wavelength and therefore a lower frequency. A low frequency will result in a lower pitch. (*1 mark will be awarded for correct scientific terminology*)

**(c)** Red-shift

**(d)** It will be blue-shifted.

**(e)** That it is expanding.

**14. (a)** The further away the galaxy, the faster it is moving away from us.

**(b) Any one from:** Galaxies are very far away, making them difficult to study; In the 1920s, technology was not as good as it is today.

**(c)** The Universe began from a very small initial point with a massive explosion; and has been expanding ever since.

**(d)** Cosmic microwave background radiation

**(e) Any two from:** It does not fully explain all the evidence available about the Universe; It does not explain how the Big Bang happened, it just says it did; Many people believe the Universe was created by God.

**15. (a) (i)** False
**(ii)** True
**(iii)** False
**(iv)** False

**(b)** Ultraviolet radiation is absorbed by the nucleus of cells; causing it (DNA) to mutate.

**(c) (i)** Sunscreen
**(ii)** Staying indoors
**(iii)** 200 minutes.

**16. (a)** Microwaves

**(b) Any two from:** The rays are absorbed by water molecules; The heat produced may damage or kill cells; The rays could perhaps cause cancer.

**4.** Crude oil is a finite resource, which means that there is a limited supply of it. Ethanol and hydrogen are possible alternatives.

**(a)** Give **one** reason **for** and **against** using ethanol and hydrogen as fuels. Write your answers in the table below. (4 marks)

| Fuel | Advantage | Disadvantage |
|---|---|---|
| Ethanol | **(i)** | **(ii)** |
| Hydrogen | **(iii)** | **(iv)** |

**(b)** *In this question you will be assessed on using good English, organising information clearly and using scientific terms where appropriate.*

How is hydrogen made? What are the disadvantages of using hydrogen as an alternative to petrol and diesel for cars? (6 marks)

**5.** Crude oil is often found in the Earth's crust. Why does this cause a problem? (1 mark)

**6.** Write down **one** way in which the environment is affected when oil is extracted. (1 mark)

**7.** What particular problems are there with extracting oil from under the sea? (1 mark)

**8.** Ethanol has been put forward as an alternative fuel to crude oil.

**(a)** Briefly describe the process by which ethanol is produced using renewable and non-renewable sources.

**(i)** Using renewable sources. (2 marks)

**(ii)** Using non-renewable sources. (2 marks)

**(b) (i)** Give **two advantages** of using renewable sources to produce ethanol. (2 marks)

**(ii)** Give **one disadvantage** of using renewable sources to produce ethanol. (1 mark)

**(c) (i)** Give **two advantages** of using non-renewable sources to produce ethanol. (2 marks)

**(ii)** Give **one disadvantage** of using non-renewable sources to produce ethanol. (1 mark)

**(Total: .......... / 45 marks)**

**1.** **(a)** Draw the displayed formula for **decane** $C_{10}H_{22}$ in the box below. (1 mark)

**(b)** If decane is heated in the presence of a catalyst, the following reaction takes place:

$$C_{10}H_{22} \longrightarrow C_aH_b + C_2H_4$$

Work out the values of $a$ and $b$ in the formula $C_aH_b$. (2 marks)

**(c)** One of the products of cracking is a shorter-chain alkane. What type of hydrocarbon compound is the other product? (1 mark)

**(d)** The diagram below shows the apparatus used for cracking liquid paraffin in the laboratory. Complete the diagram by adding in the labels. (4 marks)

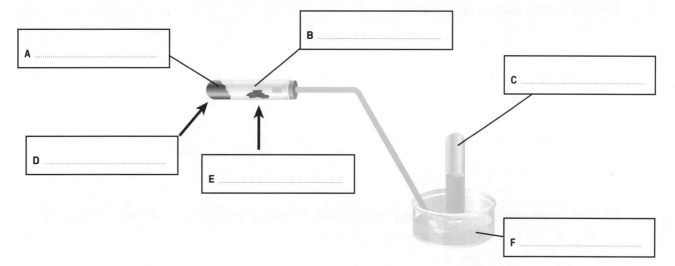

A ..............................................

B ..............................................

C ..............................................

D ..............................................

E ..............................................

F ..............................................

**2.** **(a)** There is another set of hydrocarbons called alkenes. Their names all end in −ene. Which of the following compounds is not an alkene? Circle the correct answer. (1 mark)

**propene**     **ethene**     **butene**     **pentene**     **methane**

**(b)** Alkenes are unsaturated hydrocarbons. What does the term **unsaturated** mean? (1 mark)

........................................................................................................................................................

........................................................................................................................................................

**(c)** Fill in the empty spaces in the table below. (4 marks)

| Name of Hydrocarbon | Propane | (i) .................................... |
|---|---|---|
| Formula | (ii) .................................... | $C_3H_6$ |
| Structural Formula | (iii) | (iv) |

**3.** Write down **two** uses of ethanol. (2 marks)

........................................................................................................................................................

........................................................................................................................................................

........................................................................................................................................................

**4.** **(a)** What makes alkenes very reactive? (1 mark)

........................................................................................................................................................

**(b)** Briefly explain how alkenes react to form polymers in polymerisation. (3 marks)

........................................................................................................................................................

........................................................................................................................................................

........................................................................................................................................................

**(c)** Many molecules of ethene can be joined together to make poly(ethene). What has to happen to each ethene molecule in order for this to take place? (1 mark)

........................................................................................................................................................

........................................................................................................................................................

**5.** Complete the following equation to show how three molecules of ethene join together to form part of a poly(ethene) molecule. (1 mark)

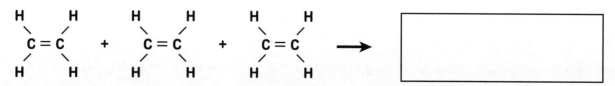

**6.** **(a)** Draw the structural formula for a poly(ethene) molecule containing 'n' molecules of ethene. (1 mark)

**(b)** What polymer would be made by reacting together molecules of chloroethene? (1 mark)

........................................................................................................................................................................

**7.** Some of the products of cracking crude oil can be used to make polymers.

**(a)** Complete the following sentences about polymers using the words from the box. (4 marks)

| polymerisation | large | plastic | chains |
|---|---|---|---|

Polymers are very ........................................ molecules. Lots of polymer ........................................

together make a ........................................ . The reaction that makes polymers from monomers is

called ........................................ .

**(b)** Draw a line to match each monomer in list A to the correct polymer in list B. (4 marks)

List A | List B

| List A | List B |
|---|---|
| ethene | poly(styrene) |
| propene | poly(vinyl chloride) |
| styrene | poly(propene) |
| chloroethene | poly(ethene) |

(c) Poly(ethene) and polystyrene have different properties. Why is this likely to be? (2 marks)

......................................................................................................................................

......................................................................................................................................

(d) Biodegradable means 'something that will rot'. Many polymers are not biodegradable. What problem would this cause for the environment? (1 mark)

......................................................................................................................................

(e) What is a good way to reduce environmental problems when using objects made from polymers? (1 mark)

......................................................................................................................................

8.   The equation below shows the polymerisation of propene to form polypropene.

$$n\ C_3H_6 \longrightarrow \left[ \begin{array}{ccc} H & H & H \\ | & | & | \\ C & - C & - C \\ | & | & | \\ H & H & H \end{array} \right]_n$$

What conditions are needed for this reaction to happen? (2 marks)

......................................................................................................................................

......................................................................................................................................

9.   Read the passage about making slime and answer the questions.

> Elliott made some slime by adding poly(ethanol) to a solution of sodium tetraborate. The slime that he made is an unusual material because it has some of the properties of a liquid and some of the properties of a solid. It can be poured, but it bounces if dropped on the floor. When Elliott mixed the substances, the sodium tetraborate formed cross-links between the polymer chains. Some of the cross-links are chemical bonds and some are intermolecular forces involving water molecules. Lots of water molecules are held between the polymer chains and these give the slime its flexibility and fluidity.

(a) Describe a molecule of a typical polymer. (1 mark)

......................................................................................................................................

......................................................................................................................................

(b) Suggest why the slime that Elliott made has the properties of both a solid and a liquid. (1 mark)

......................................................................................................................................

......................................................................................................................................

**(c)** Suggest **one** method that you could use to modify the properties of the slime. (1 mark)

........................................................................................................................................................

........................................................................................................................................................

**10.** Look at the table of polymers and some of their uses.

| polythene | polystyrene | polyester | nylon |
|---|---|---|---|
| can be made into a thin sheet | can be expanded to a light structure | can be made into a fibre | can be made into a fibre |
| flexible | rigid | flexible | flexible |
| waterproof | waterproof | waterproof | waterproof |

**(a)** Which polymer has a rigid structure? (1 mark)

........................................................................................................................................................

**(b)** Which **two** polymers can be made into fibres? (1 mark)

........................................................................................................................................................

**(c)** Which polymer is used for plastic bags? (1 mark)

........................................................................................................................................................

**(d)** Which polymer is used for damage protection in packaging and for insulation? (1 mark)

........................................................................................................................................................

**(e)** Which **two** polymers are used in clothing? (1 mark)

........................................................................................................................................................

**(f)** GORE-TEX[R] is a modern fabric that is waterproof, but also 'breathes'. Write down **one** advantage of waterproof clothing. (1 mark)

........................................................................................................................................................

**(g)** Write down **one** advantage of breathable clothing. (1 mark)

........................................................................................................................................................

**(Total:** ............ **/ 48 marks)**

**1.** Useful oils can be extracted from vegetables, fruits and seeds.

**(a)** Name the **two** processes by which oil can be extracted from plant material. (2 marks)

......................................................................................................................................

......................................................................................................................................

**(b)** Write down **two** vegetable oils that can be turned into fuels. (2 marks)

......................................................................................................................................

......................................................................................................................................

**(c)** What makes vegetable oils suitable for making fuels? (1 mark)

......................................................................................................................................

**(d)** Give **three** reasons why biodiesel is a better choice than petrol or normal diesel for a
transport fuel. (3 marks)

......................................................................................................................................

......................................................................................................................................

......................................................................................................................................

**(e)** Give **three** reasons why biodiesel is not as good a choice as petrol or normal diesel for a
transport fuel. (3 marks)

......................................................................................................................................

......................................................................................................................................

......................................................................................................................................

**2.** **(a)** Complete the following statements: (2 marks)

**(i)** Vegetable oils can be detected using b ........................................ w ........................................ .

**(ii)** A mixture of oil and water is called an e ........................................ .

**(b) (i)** Draw the structural formula equation for the reaction of ethene and bromine water. (2 marks)

**(ii)** What happens to the bromine atoms in this reaction? (1 mark)

3.  **(a)** Why does oil not dissolve in water? (1 mark)

**(b)** Why would you add mustard to a salad dressing made from oil and vinegar? (1 mark)

4.  The box shows some different fats and oils. Complete the sentences by underlining the **correct** word.

(4 marks)

| | |
|---|---|
| **Butter** | **Rapeseed oil** |
| | **Olive oil** |
| **Margarine** | |
| | **Lard** |
| **Fish oil** | |
| | **Sunflower oil** |

**(a)** All the animal fats listed are **unsaturated / saturated** apart from **fish oil / lard**.

**(b)** All the unsaturated fats are **solid / liquid** at room temperature.

**(c)** Saturated fats, such as **corn oil / butter**, have **no / some** double bonds.

**(d)** **Sunflower / olive** oil is a polyunsaturated fat. This means it has **one / more than one** double bond for each molecule of fat.

**5.** **(a)** Explain why fats and oils are an important food group. (1 mark)

**(b)** State **one** health risk associated with eating too many saturated fats. (1 mark)

**6.** The more carbon to carbon double bonds there are in a molecule, the lower its melting point is.

**(a)** How could you increase the melting point of an oil to produce a solid fat? (2 marks)

**(b)** Write the word equation for this reaction. (1 mark)

**7.** **(a)** Write down **two** advantages of using additives in foods. (2 marks)

**(b)** Write down **two** disadvantages of using additives in foods. (2 marks)

(Total: ........ / 31 marks)

**Higher Tier**

8. What is the name of the process shown in the equation below? (1 mark)

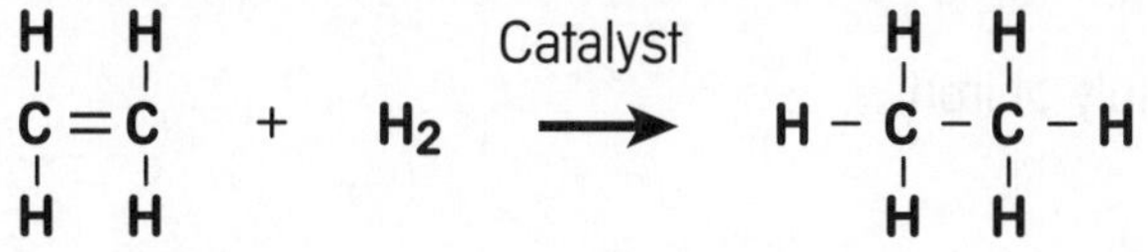

$$\underset{\underset{H}{|}}{\overset{\overset{H}{|}}{C}} = \underset{\underset{H}{|}}{\overset{\overset{H}{|}}{C}} \quad + \quad H_2 \quad \xrightarrow{\text{Catalyst}} \quad H - \underset{\underset{H}{|}}{\overset{\overset{H}{|}}{C}} - \underset{\underset{H}{|}}{\overset{\overset{H}{|}}{C}} - H$$

(Total: _____ / 1 mark)

1. Using the information listed below, make a scale drawing of the Earth. **(4 marks)**

   - The centre of the Earth is 6370km down.
   - The continental crust is 25km thick at its thinnest point and 90km thick at its thickest point.
   - Underneath the lithosphere is the main mantle.
   - The outer core starts 2900km down.
   - The outer core is liquid and made mainly of iron.
   - The inner core starts 5155km down.
   - The inner core is solid and made mainly of iron.

2. Describe the **two** pieces of evidence relating to the east coast of South America and the west coast of Africa that led scientists such as Alfred Wegener to believe that the features of the Earth's surface were not caused by shrinkage, as originally thought. **(4 marks)**

3. **(a)** Briefly describe the main points in Wegener's theory. **(3 marks)**

   **(b)** What could Wegener's theory not explain? **(1 mark)**

**4.** What natural hazards commonly occur where two tectonic plates meet? (1 mark)

_____

**5.** Why do you think it is hard for scientists to predict when these natural hazards will happen? (2 marks)

_____

_____

**6.** Explain, using the theory of how tectonic plates move, why earthquakes occur along the east coast of North America. (2 marks)

_____

_____

_____

**7.** **(a)** What is a constructive plate margin? (2 marks)

_____

_____

_____

**(b)** What is a destructive plate margin? (2 marks)

_____

_____

_____

**(c)** Label the **two** different plate margins shown in the diagram below. One is **constructive** and one is **destructive**. (2 marks)

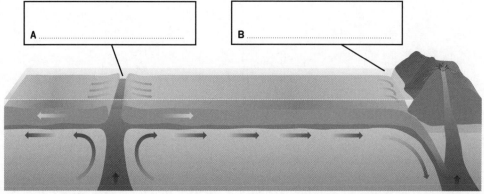

A ...........................................

B ...........................................

**8.** Up until the early 1900s, nobody had put forward any evidence to contradict the theory of the Earth shrinking.

**(a)** In 1915, who proposed the idea that led to the development of modern tectonic theory?     (1 mark)

......................................................................................................................................................

**(b)** Summarise the explanations that he proposed.     (2 marks)

......................................................................................................................................................

......................................................................................................................................................

**(c)** In the 1950s, new evidence was discovered that supported the theory. Although some parts of the theory were found to be incorrect, it was generally well founded.

Briefly describe the Tectonic Theory that was proposed as a result.     (2 marks)

......................................................................................................................................................

......................................................................................................................................................

......................................................................................................................................................

**9.** **(a)** Where on the Earth's crust do the majority of volcanoes and earthquakes happen?     (1 mark)

......................................................................................................................................................

**(b)** Explain why tectonic plates float on top of the mantle.     (1 mark)

......................................................................................................................................................

**(c)** Why does lava from volcanoes not form large crystals?     (1 mark)

......................................................................................................................................................

**10.** **(a)** The percentage of carbon dioxide in the atmosphere is increasing. Write down **two** reasons why this is happening. *(2 marks)*

(i) ................................................... (ii) ...................................................

**(b)** Explain why the total amount of nitrogen doesn't change. *(2 marks)*

...................................................................................................................................

...................................................................................................................................

**11.** **(a)** Complete the table below to explain how human activity impacts on the atmosphere. *(3 marks)*

| Human activity | Pollutant | Impact on the atmosphere |
|---|---|---|
| (i) ............................... ............................... | Sulfur dioxide Carbon dioxide | Sulfur dioxide can form acid rain, which erodes buildings and adds acid to lakes and soils. |
| Population growth and deforestation | Carbon dioxide | (ii) ............................... |
| (iii) ............................... ............................... ............................... | Carbon monoxide | Carbon monoxide eventually reacts with oxygen to form carbon dioxide. This increases the amount of greenhouse gases leading to global warming. |

**(b)** Consider **one** of the human activities in the table above in more detail. Summarise the impact that the activity has had on the atmosphere. *(2 marks)*

...................................................................................................................................

...................................................................................................................................

...................................................................................................................................

**(c)** How can the amount of pollutants in the atmosphere be reduced? Give **three** ways in which we can help. *(3 marks)*

...................................................................................................................................

...................................................................................................................................

...................................................................................................................................

**12.** Air is a mixture of gases. The pie chart shows the percentages, by volume, of the main gases in dry air.

**(a)** Complete the chart by adding the names of these **three** gases. (3 marks)

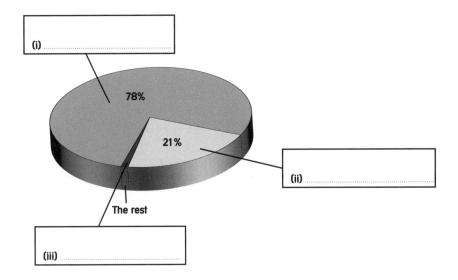

(i) ..............................

78%

21%

(ii) ..............................

The rest

(iii) ..............................

**(b)** The chart shows the composition of the Earth's atmosphere as it is today. Put a number next to each of the statements to show the correct order **(1–7)** in which they happened to result in the composition of the atmosphere today. (4 marks)

(i) After cooling down slightly, a thin crust formed. ..............................

(ii) The first plants evolved. ..............................

(iii) Water vapour condensed and the oceans were formed. ..............................

(iv) Complex life forms appeared. ..............................

(v) Photosynthesis by plants built up the level of oxygen and the ozone layer formed.

..............................

(vi) The atmosphere is about 80% nitrogen and 20% oxygen. ..............................

(vii)The surface of the Earth was molten and there was lots of volcanic activity.

..............................

**13.** **(a)** Look at the diagrams and use the words in the box to complete the table. (4 marks)

| combustion | respiration | photosynthesis | oxygen | carbon dioxide |

| Name of process | Gas made | Gas used up |
|---|---|---|
| 1 | | |
| 2 | | |
| 3 | | |
| 4 | | |

**(b)** Suggest why arrow 4 in the diagram is much thicker than the other three. (1 mark)

**(c)** Explain why carbon dioxide is important for life. (2 marks)

**(d)** Explain why the amounts of oxygen and carbon dioxide would remain stable in the absence of human activity. (1 mark)

**(e)** The total amount of nitrogen in the atmosphere does not change. Explain why. (1 mark)

(Total: ............ / 59 marks)

1. Houses in warm countries are often painted white to help keep them cool in the summer. Draw a line from one sentence in list A to one sentence in list B to explain why this works. (1 mark)

**List A**

| |
|---|
| Heat energy from the Sun reaches the houses by thermal radiation. |

| |
|---|
| Heat energy from the Sun reaches the houses by conduction. |

| |
|---|
| Heat energy from the Sun reaches the houses by convection. |

**List B**

| |
|---|
| White is a poor conductor of heat. |

| |
|---|
| Black is a good absorber of thermal radiation. |

| |
|---|
| White is a poor absorber of thermal radiation. |

2. The diagrams below show four different types of coffee cup used by a take-away coffee house. Each cup holds the same amount of coffee.

A          B          C          D

**(a)** Which type of cup would keep the drink hottest? Explain why. (3 marks)

_____

_____

_____

**(b)** Which type of cup would cool quickest? Explain why. (3 marks)

_____

_____

_____

3. All matter is made of particles. In the spaces below, sketch the particle arrangement for the different states of matter. You do not need to draw more than nine particles for each diagram. (3 marks)

| | | |
|---|---|---|
| Solid | Liquid | Gas |

4. *In this question you will be assessed on using good English, organising information clearly and using scientific terms where appropriate.* (6 marks)

In terms of particle movement and energy, explain what happens as a solid is heated to become a liquid.

......................................................................................................

......................................................................................................

......................................................................................................

......................................................................................................

......................................................................................................

5. *In this question you will be assessed on using good English, organising information clearly and using scientific terms where appropriate.* (6 marks)

In terms of particle movement and energy, explain what happens as a liquid is heated to become a gas.

......................................................................................................

......................................................................................................

......................................................................................................

......................................................................................................

......................................................................................................

6. Before electric fans were invented, mines used to be ventilated by lighting a fire at the bottom of one of the shafts.

**(a)** Add **two** arrows, one labelled **hot air** and the other **cold air**, to show movement of air in and out of the mine. (2 marks)

**(b)** What name is given to this process? (1 mark)

.................................................................................................................................................

**(c)** Explain the movement of air shown in the diagram. For full marks your answer should refer to particles in the air. (5 marks)

.................................................................................................................................................

.................................................................................................................................................

.................................................................................................................................................

.................................................................................................................................................

.................................................................................................................................................

.................................................................................................................................................

.................................................................................................................................................

**7.** In a supermarket, the freezers do not usually have lids.

Why doesn't the cold air escape out of the top of the freezer? (2 marks)

........................................................................................................................

........................................................................................................................

**8.** Heat transfer in solids takes place by conduction.

**(a)** Describe the process of conduction in terms of particle movement. (2 marks)

........................................................................................................................

........................................................................................................................

**(b)** Metals are better conductors of heat than non-metals. What feature of metals makes them better conductors than non-metals? (1 mark)

........................................................................................................................

**9.** Baked Alaska is a dessert that is made by placing ice cream on a layer of sponge and then coating with fluffy air-filled white meringue. Once this has been prepared, it is baked in an oven for 10 minutes. After baking, the ice cream has not melted.

Use your knowledge of conduction, convection and/or radiation to explain as fully as you can why the ice cream does not melt. (4 marks)

........................................................................................................................

........................................................................................................................

........................................................................................................................

........................................................................................................................

........................................................................................................................

**(Total: ............ /39 marks)**

1. The following information was included in a newspaper advertisement for a tumble dryer.

> Traditional tumble dryers draw in dry air and heat it before passing it through the tumbler. The hot, humid air produced is usually vented outside to make room for more dry air to continue the drying process. The traditional design makes no effort to recycle the heat.
>
> Our new heat pump dryer uses the energy from the exhaust gases to heat the incoming air, resulting in a 33% reduction in energy use; this would save the average family £40 per year.

**(a)** A tumble dryer works by evaporating the water from the clothes. What **two** features of the air used in a tumble dryer make it effective at drying clothes? (2 marks)

.......................................................................................................................................................

.......................................................................................................................................................

**(b)** The new heat pump dryer costs £120 more than a traditional tumble dryer. In terms of energy savings, how long is the payback time for an average family? (1 mark)

.......................................................................................................................................................

.......................................................................................................................................................

**(c)** Suggest **one** reason, other than saving money on fuel bills, why people may be encouraged to choose the new heat pump dryer. (1 mark)

.......................................................................................................................................................

.......................................................................................................................................................

2. On a hot day, dogs will often be seen panting, even if they are not running around. Explain how the evaporation of water from a dog's tongue helps the dog to cool down. (3 marks)

.......................................................................................................................................................

.......................................................................................................................................................

.......................................................................................................................................................

**3.** The table below shows different methods of insulating a home.

| Method | Cost | Annual saving | Payback time (years) |
|---|---|---|---|
| Double glazing | £4000 | £200 | (i) |
| Loft insulation | £250 | £125 | (ii) |
| Cavity wall insulation | £400 | £40 | (iii) |
| Draft proofing | £60 | £20 | (iv) |

**(a)** Complete the table to show the payback time. (4 marks)

**(b)** Which method is the most cost-effective? (1 mark)

**4.** A householder is considering installing double glazing and is comparing the energy saving of different types. The U-value of a material indicates how good an insulator it is. A high U-value means that heat can flow through it quickly.

The table shows the U-values for different double glazing products.

| Option | Type of glass | U-VALUE | |
|---|---|---|---|
| | | 10mm gap | 20mm gap |
| 1 | 4mm normal | 3.2 | 3.3 |
| 2 | 4mm reflective | 2.4 | 2.3 |
| 3 | 6mm normal | 2.5 | 2.6 |
| 4 | 6mm reflective | 1.8 | 1.8 |

**(a)** What conclusion can be drawn about the size of the gap between the panes of glass and the energy efficiency? (1 mark)

**(b)** What conclusion can be drawn about the type of glass and the energy efficiency?          (2 marks)

**(c)** Apart from efficiency, suggest **one** other factor that the householder may consider when deciding which type of double glazing to install.          (1 mark)

**5.**     The diagram shows a roof-mounted solar water heating system designed for domestic use. The solar collector is black.

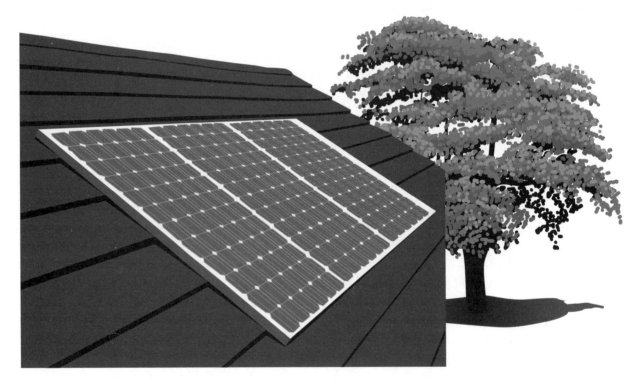

**(a)** Why is the solar collector black?          (1 mark)

**(b)** The system is designed to feed hot water to a tank connected to a gas boiler. Suggest a reason for the boiler.          (1 mark)

**(c)** A 1m$^2$ panel is capable of supplying 5.25MJ of energy per day. To provide enough hot water for an average family, the heater needs to raise the temperature of 100kg of water from 20°C to 70°C.

How big would the solar panel need to be to provide enough hot water for an average family?

The specific heat capacity of water is 4200J/kg°C.

Select the correct formula from the equation sheet and show all your working out.          (5 marks)

6.    Read the article below.

---

**Regenerative braking lends hope to electric cars.**

Replacing traditional friction brakes with electromagnetic brakes will allow electric cars to have increased range by reducing energy waste during braking. One of the main problems with electric vehicles has been battery life. Regenerative braking uses the kinetic energy of the vehicle to produce electrical energy that recharges the batteries when the vehicle slows down.

---

**(a)** What is the main output energy of friction brakes?                                   (1 mark)

**(b)** Electric trains on the London underground have used regenerative braking for many years. What has been the main advantage of fitting these brakes?                                   (1 mark)

**(c)** Regenerative brakes recover two thirds of the input energy, with the remainder being converted to heat and sound. Sketch and label a Sankey diagram for regenerative brakes. **(4 marks)**

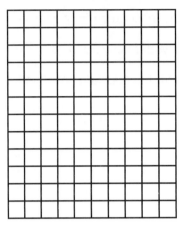

7. Hybrid cars use regenerative braking. This allows them to achieve an average fuel efficiency of 10 miles per litre. A standard petrol car will average 6 miles per litre.

**(a)** If a car owner drives 9000 miles in a year, how much fuel would he save each year by switching to a hybrid car? **(4 marks)**

**(b)** Use your answer to part **(a)** to calculate the following:

If petrol costs £1.25 per litre, how much more will it cost per year to fuel a normal petrol car? **(2 marks)**

**(c)** A typical hybrid car will cost £3000 more than a standard petrol car. In terms of fuel savings, what is the payback time of switching to using a hybrid car? **(2 marks)**

**(Total: ............ / 37 marks)**

1. **List A** shows three devices that all transfer energy. (3 marks)

   Draw **three** straight lines from list A to list B to match each device to the useful energy it produces.

   **List A**

   | Car |

   | Kettle |

   | Torch |

   **List B**

   | Light |

   | Sound |

   | Kinetic |

   | Heat |

   | Electrical |

2. The table shows some information about an electric drill. Some information has been left out.

   **(a)** Complete the information in the table. (2 marks)

   | Form of energy input | **(i)** |
   |---|---|
   | Form of useful energy output | **(ii)** |
   | Wasted energy | Heat and sound |
   | Power rating | 500W |
   | Efficiency | 60% |

   **(b)** Calculate the useful power output of the drill. (2 marks)

   **(c)** Half of the wasted energy is heat and the other half is sound. Calculate the sound energy wasted per second. (3 marks)

**(d)** Which of the following statements about the energy from the drill is incorrect. Put a cross in the box next to the incorrect statement. (1 mark)

| | |
|---|---|
| It spreads out and becomes more difficult to use. | |
| It disappears. | |
| It makes the surroundings warmer. | |

**3.** A compact fluorescent lamp produces 20J of energy in the form of light for every 50J of electrical energy supplied.

**(a)** Calculate the efficiency of the lamp. (1 mark)

......................................................................................................................................

**(b)** Use the grid below to draw a labelled Sankey diagram for the above lamp. Label the input and output energies and their values. (4 marks)

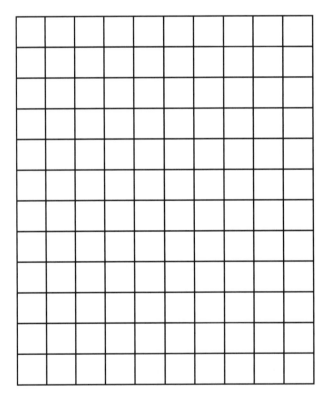

**(c)** The compact fluorescent lamp is four times as efficient as an old-style filament lamp. How efficient is the filament lamp? (1 mark)

......................................................................................................................................

**(d)** How much energy in the form of heat is produced by a filament lamp with an input energy of 200J? (2 marks)

......................................................................................................................................

**(e)** Replacing all the filament lamps in a house with compact fluorescents would cost £10 and would save £20 per year. Use the idea of payback time to explain whether this is a cost-effective energy-saving measure. (2 marks)

........................................................................................................................................................

........................................................................................................................................................

........................................................................................................................................................

**4.** This Sankey diagram shows the energy transfer from a petrol-powered car.

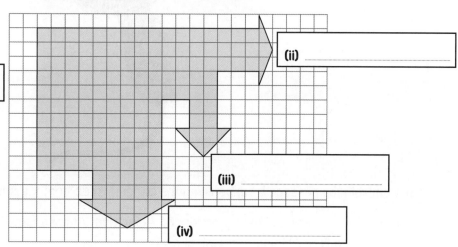

**(i)** ........................................

**(ii)** ........................................

**(iii)** ........................................

**(iv)** ........................................

**(a)** Fill in the blank labels on the diagram using the words listed below. (4 marks)

**Chemical energy**      **Kinetic energy**      **Sound energy**      **Thermal energy**

**(b)** Use the diagram to work out how much energy is usefully transferred if the car has an input energy of 3000J. (2 marks)

........................................................................................................................................................

........................................................................................................................................................

**(c)** What is the efficiency of the car? (2 marks)

........................................................................................................................................................

........................................................................................................................................................

5.  Complete the left- and right-hand columns in the table below to show the main energy transfers that occur in different situations. (5 marks)

| Input energy | Situation | Useful output energy |
|---|---|---|
| (a) ............................... | Walking uphill | (b) ............................... |
| (c) ............................... | Sliding down a slide | (d) ............................... |
| (e) ............................... | Firing a catapult | (f) ............................... |
| (g) ............................... | Fireworks sparklers | (h) ............................... |

6.  The picture shows a hairdryer that blows warm air.

(a) Complete the passage by underlining the correct words from the options provided. (3 marks)

A hairdryer is designed to convert **kinetic / electrical / heat** energy into **heat / sound / electrical** energy and **light / kinetic / chemical** energy.

(b) The hairdryer has an input power of 1200W. If it takes three minutes to dry a person's hair, how much energy does it use? Give your answer in joules. (3 marks)

......................................................................................................................

......................................................................................................................

......................................................................................................................

(c) The hairdryer is 90% efficient, with the wasted energy being lost as sound. How much sound energy is produced? (2 marks)

......................................................................................................................

......................................................................................................................

**7.** The table below shows the energy transfers from a number of household appliances. Complete the table by filling in the empty cells. The first row has been completed for you. (4 marks)

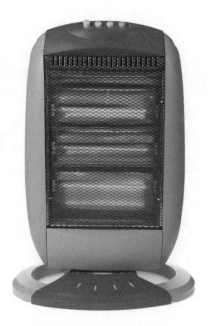 

| Device | Input energy | Main useful output energy | Main waste energy |
|--------|-------------|---------------------------|-------------------|
| Television | Electrical | Light and sound | Heat |
| Radio | Electrical | (a) | (b) |
| Light bulb | (c) | (d) | Heat |
| Electric fire | Electrical | (e) | (f) |

**8.** Electrical energy usage in the home is not measured in joules.

**(a)** What unit is used to measure domestic electricity usage? (1 mark)

........................................................................................................................................

**(b)** A family watches television for three hours per day.
If the television is 500W, what is the weekly energy usage? (3 marks)

........................................................................................................................................

........................................................................................................................................

........................................................................................................................................

**9.** The following is an extract from a magazine article about different types of light bulbs.

With the upcoming ban on inefficient filament bulbs, the market has opened up for a range of lighting solutions with the main contenders being LED lighting and Compact Fluorescent (low energy) bulbs.

**(a)** Suggest **two** reasons why filament bulbs are going to be banned. (2 marks)

............................................................................................................

............................................................................................................

**(b)** The table below compares the three types of bulb, all of which provide the same amount of light.

| Type of bulb | Cost per bulb | Bulb lifetime | Electricity usage in 30 000 hours | Cost for 30 000 hours' use (£) |
|---|---|---|---|---|
| Filament lamp | 50p | 1000 hours | 3000kWh | A |
| Compact fluorescent | £1 | 6000 hours | 600kWh | B |
| LED | £25 | 30 000 hours | 100kWh | C |

**(i)** Using the information in the table, which bulb is the most efficient? (1 mark)

............................................................................................................

**(ii)** Electricity costs are 6p per kWh. Complete the table to show the cost for 30 000 hours' use. (3 marks)

**(iii)** By looking at the bulb cost, bulb lifetime and the electricity usage, which bulb is the most cost-effective? (1 mark)

............................................................................................................

**(iv)** Despite the savings, many people do not choose the most cost-effective bulb. Suggest why. (1 mark)

............................................................................................................

**10.** The diagram shows a typical electricity bill from a company that has an economy charge for night-time use and a normal charge for daytime use. These two charges are added together to give the total cost.

---

**REB** Regional **Electricity** Board

Mr R. Jones
273 Dove Street
Southampton
SW15 WFK

**Electricity Statement. Period: 01.01.06 – 01.04.06** No standing charge

| Present reading | Previous reading | kWh used | Cost per kWh (p) | Charge amount (£) |
|---|---|---|---|---|
| 12898 (economy) | 12640 (economy) | A | 7.0 | B |
| 30803 | 30332 | C | 9.0 | D |
| | | | Total | E |

Regional Electricity Board, Anchor House, Ingleby Street, Southampton SW15 TNE  **Telephone:** 01445 680180 **Fax:** 01445 680180 **Email:** info@reb.co.uk **Web:** www.reb.co.uk

---

**(a)** Fill in the empty cells labelled **A–E** on the bill to find the energy used and total cost. (5 marks)

**(b)** A different company claims that switching to them could result in cheaper bills.

    **(i)** Who should a home owner check with to see if they should switch?
    Circle the correct answer. (1 mark)

      A salesman from the new company      An independent website

      A television advert      Their existing electricity provider

    **(ii)** Explain your answer to part **(i)** (2 marks)

---

**11.** An electric blender transfers electrical energy into kinetic, heat and sound energy.

**(a)** What is the useful energy output? (1 mark)

**(b)** After the waste energy is given off, what happens to it? (1 mark)

**(c)** The blender is used for two minutes. If the blender has an input power of 400W and is 75% efficient, how much waste energy is given off in this time? (4 marks)

12. The table below gives the power rating and daily usage for a number of different appliances.

| Appliance | Power rating | Total hours used per day |
|---|---|---|
| Kettle | 2000W | 1 |
| Fridge | 250W | 24 |
| Television | 500W | 6 |
| Oven | 5000W | 1 |

**(a)** Which appliance uses the least energy per hour? (1 mark)

**(b)** How many kilowatt hours of energy are used by the fridge every day? (2 marks)

**(c)** If the cost per unit is eight pence, what is the total daily cost to run the four appliances? (6 marks)

(Total: ........... / 81 marks)

1. Around three quarters of the electricity used in the UK is generated by burning coal or gas. However, reserves are limited and the UK already imports fuel from overseas.

   **(a)** Some people suggest that we need to build more nuclear power stations so that we do not have to rely on imported gas. Which of the following are **not** an argument in favour of building nuclear power stations? Tick the **two** correct answers. (2 marks)

   They have a high output. ☐

   They have a long start-up time. ☐

   They do not produce greenhouse gases. ☐

   Waste materials remain dangerous for a very long time. ☐

   **(b)** Which **two** elements are used for nuclear fuel? (2 marks)

   .........................................................................................................................................................

   .........................................................................................................................................................

   **(c)** What process takes place inside a nuclear reactor to release energy? (1 mark)

   .........................................................................................................................................................

   **(d)** Outline the similarities between using coal and nuclear fuel in the process to generate electricity. (3 marks)

   .........................................................................................................................................................

   .........................................................................................................................................................

   .........................................................................................................................................................

   **(e)** Name **two** of the main gases produced by burning coal and explain why these gases are undesirable. (4 marks)

   .........................................................................................................................................................

   .........................................................................................................................................................

   .........................................................................................................................................................

   .........................................................................................................................................................

2. To meet increasing energy demand, the UK is looking to renewable energy sources.

   **(a)** What is the difference between a renewable and non-renewable energy resource? (2 marks)

   .........................................................................................................................................................

   .........................................................................................................................................................

**(b)** Which of the resources in the list is not renewable? Circle the correct answer.　　(1 mark)

Solar　　　　　　　　　　　　　　　　Wind

Nuclear　　　　　　　　　　　　　　　Biomass (e.g. wood)

**(c)** A large offshore wind farm is being built in the North Sea off the east coast of the UK. It will need to be connected to the National Grid with electricity pylons, causing protests by some residents who claim the pylons will spoil the view.

**(i)** Outline **three** advantages of using above-ground pylons instead of underground cables.

(3 marks)

.................................................................................................................................................................

.................................................................................................................................................................

.................................................................................................................................................................

.................................................................................................................................................................

**(ii)** Give **two** disadvantages of above-ground electricity pylons.　　(2 marks)

.................................................................................................................................................................

.................................................................................................................................................................

.................................................................................................................................................................

**(d)** A large wind turbine can generate enough energy for 1000 homes, but it is not practical as the UK's only energy solution. Explain why other sources of energy are also needed.　　(2 marks)

.................................................................................................................................................................

.................................................................................................................................................................

.................................................................................................................................................................

**3.** The diagram below shows how carbon capture is being used to reduce $CO_2$ emissions.

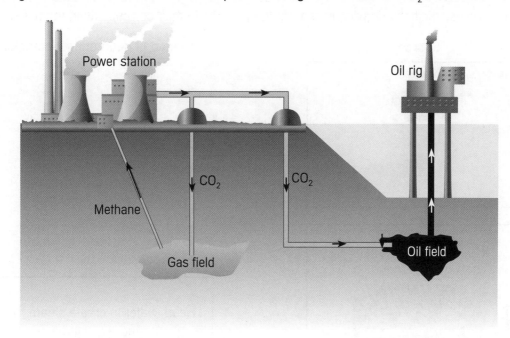

**(a)** Why is carbon capture considered important in fossil fuel power stations? (1 mark)

........................................................................................................................................

**(b)** Use the diagram to explain how carbon capture can help with the extraction of existing oil and gas reserves. (2 marks)

........................................................................................................................................

........................................................................................................................................

........................................................................................................................................

........................................................................................................................................

**(c)** The diagram above shows a gas-fired power station. These have a shorter start-up time than most other power stations. Use an example to explain how this is useful. (3 marks)

........................................................................................................................................

........................................................................................................................................

........................................................................................................................................

**(d)** In addition to the short start-up time, give another advantage of gas-fired power stations over other fossil fuel power stations. (1 mark)

........................................................................................................................................

4. The pictures below show different methods of generating electricity. Match each picture to its method of generating electricity by drawing lines from the pictures to their corresponding methods. **(5 marks)**

**Source**

Nuclear

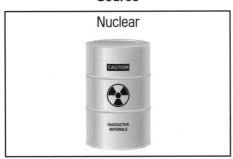

Solar cells

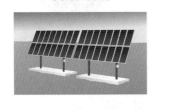

Wind

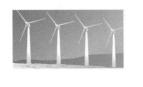

Biofuels

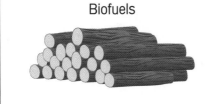

Hydroelectric dam

**Method of generating electricity**

Heats water to create steam that drives turbines

Drives turbines directly

Produces electricity directly by converting energy from sunlight

**5.** The solar tower in Spain uses hundreds of huge mirrors to reflect sunlight onto a large tank full of water. This creates steam that is used to drive turbines.

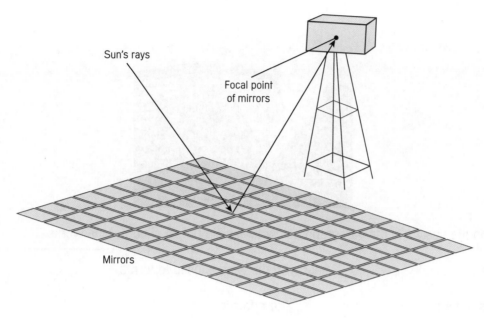

Sun's rays

Focal point
of mirrors

Mirrors

**(a)** For maximum efficiency, the tank is painted black and the mirrors are kept highly polished. Suggest why. (2 marks)

_____

_____

**(b)** The manufacturers of the solar furnace describe this as 'free energy'.

**(i)** Why could this be considered true? (1 mark)

_____

**(ii)** Why could this be considered false? (1 mark)

_____

**(c)** Although it produces no pollution, the power station still has some environmental impact. Suggest **two** ways in which it has impacted on the environment. (2 marks)

_____

_____

**(d)** Similar power stations are planned for Australia, but not the UK. Why not? (1 mark)

_____

**6.** It is now possible to purchase small wind turbines to put on the roof of your house. One of these small-scale production methods costs around £1800 and will generate electrical power at a maximum rate of 1.5KW.

**(a)** Fill in the spaces in the paragraph below to explain how a wind turbine works. (4 marks)

The ............................................ energy in the wind is used to turn a ............................................ .

This turns a ............................................ , producing ............................................ .

**(b)** Calculate how many units (kWh) of electricity one of these turbines will produce per day. (2 marks)

............................................................................................................................

............................................................................................................................

**(c)** If the wind turbine saves the householder 10p for every kWh produced, calculate the payback time in days. (4 marks)

............................................................................................................................

............................................................................................................................

............................................................................................................................

............................................................................................................................

**(d)** In practice, the payback time is much longer than the calculated value. Give **two** reasons why. (2 marks)

............................................................................................................................

............................................................................................................................

**(e)** Despite the relatively small savings, small-scale electricity generation is becoming more popular. Suggest **two** reasons why. (2 marks)

............................................................................................................................

............................................................................................................................

**7.** The diagram shows a pumped storage hydroelectric system.

Water collects in the upper reservoir and flows down pipes to the turbines and generators.

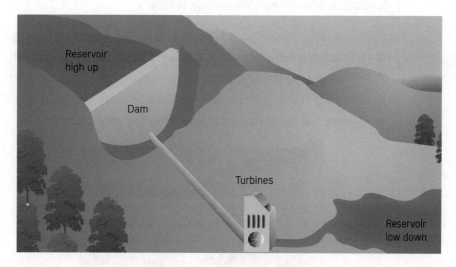

**(a)** What type of energy does the water stored in the upper reservoir contain? (1 mark)

...........................................................................................................................................................

**(b)** Explain why hydroelectric systems are good for meeting sudden peaks in demand. (2 marks)

...........................................................................................................................................................

...........................................................................................................................................................

**(c)** Explain what happens when there is a surplus of electricity. (2 marks)

...........................................................................................................................................................

...........................................................................................................................................................

**(d)** Give **two** other advantages of hydroelectric systems. (2 marks)

...........................................................................................................................................................

...........................................................................................................................................................

**(e)** The Three Gorges Dam in China is the largest hydroelectric system in the world. It generates as much energy as 18 coal-fired power stations, without producing any polluting gases, yet many people opposed its construction. Suggest why. (4 marks)

...........................................................................................................................................................

...........................................................................................................................................................

...........................................................................................................................................................

...........................................................................................................................................................

**8.** The following is an extract from a newspaper.

**Iceland, world renewable energy leader**

Although many countries are beginning to use renewable energy, the volcanically active country of Iceland is the world leader, with 81% of its energy being produced from renewable energy sources. Its hundreds of hot springs and high temperature steam fields are harnessed to provide heating across the entire country.

**(a)** What name is given to the renewable energy source described above? (1 mark)

**(b)** What is the source of this energy? (2 marks)

**9.** The diagram shows the National Grid, which is used to distribute electricity from power stations to customers.

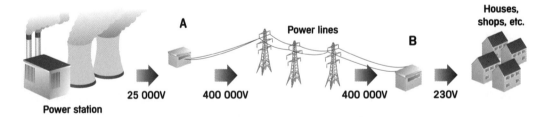

**(a)** Name parts **A** and **B** on the diagram. (2 marks)

A

B

**(b)** Part **A** increases the voltage. What effect does this have on the current and why is this important? (2 marks)

........................................................................................................................

........................................................................................................................

........................................................................................................................

**(c)** Describe the function of part **B**. (2 marks)

........................................................................................................................

........................................................................................................................

........................................................................................................................

**10.** Using transformers in the National Grid means that electricity can be transmitted from the power station to the user with very high efficiency. List **three** reasons why this is important. (3 marks)

........................................................................................................................

........................................................................................................................

........................................................................................................................

**11.** This question is about the advantages and limitations of using renewable sources to generate electricity.

**(a)** Other than biofuels/biomass, what is the main difference in the method used to drive the generators in a power station using renewable energy compared to non-renewable energy? (1 mark)

........................................................................................................................

**(b)** List **three** renewable energy sources. (3 marks)

........................................................................................................................

........................................................................................................................

**(c)** Electricity can be generated using solar energy. Describe the limitations of this method of energy production. (2 marks)

........................................................................................................................

........................................................................................................................

........................................................................................................................

**(d)** *In this question you will be assessed on using good English, organising information clearly and using scientific terms where appropriate.* (6 marks)

Compare the advantages and disadvantages of using wind and hydroelectric power stations in order to produce electricity.

_____

_____

_____

_____

_____

_____

**(e)** Give one **disadvantage** of using tidal and wave power to produce electricity. (1 mark)

_____

**(f)** Give two general **advantages** of using renewable energy sources. (2 marks)

_____

_____

(Total: _____ / 93 marks)

1. Waves can be made on a spring by holding one end and moving it up and down.

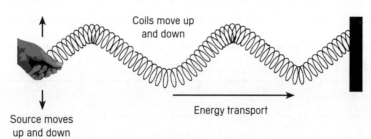

**(a)** What kind of wave is shown in the diagram? (1 mark)

**(b)** What is meant by the frequency of the wave? (1 mark)

**(c)** In the above diagram, how could the frequency of the waves produced on the spring be increased? (1 mark)

2. Waves can also be made on a spring by holding one end and moving it backwards and forwards.

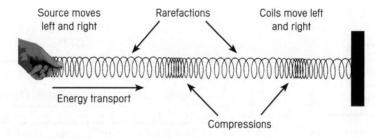

**(a)** What kind of wave is shown in the diagram? (1 mark)

**(b)** Give another example of a wave that travels in this way. (1 mark)

**(c)** What is meant by an area of rarefaction? (1 mark)

**(d)** What do all waves transfer? (1 mark)

**3.** This question is about electromagnetic waves.

**(a)** Complete the table below showing the order of the electromagnetic spectrum. (4 marks)

| **High Frequency** |
| --- |
| Gamma rays |
| **(i)** |
| **(ii)** |
| Light |
| Infrared |
| **(iii)** |
| **(iv)** |
| **Low Frequency** |

**(b)** Match the name of the process in list A with the example of where this is seen with light in list B, by drawing lines from one to the other. (3 marks)

**List A**

| Reflection |
| --- |

| Refraction |
| --- |

| Diffraction |
| --- |

**List B**

| Light changing direction leaving a swimming pool, making the pool look shallower |
| --- |

| Light bouncing off a mirror, enabling a car driver to see behind them |
| --- |

| Light bouncing off a compact disc, splitting into many different colours |
| --- |

**(c)** Mobile phones send signals using electromagnetic waves. Which type of electromagnetic wave is used? (1 mark)

**(d)** A scientist interviewed on television says he thinks that using mobile phones too much increases the risk of developing a brain tumour. What is this? (1 mark)

Circle the correct answer.

**(i)** A conclusion

**(ii)** A fact

**(iii)** An opinion

**(e)** A study on the link between mobile phones and brain tumours covered 420 000 adults over a 10-year period. The results of the study showed no correlation between the amount of mobile phone use and brain tumours. The following conclusions are suggested.

| A | Short to medium-term use by adults does not cause brain tumours. |
|---|---|
| B | Mobile phones are completely safe to use. |
| C | Children should not use mobile phones. |
| D | It is not safe for adults to use mobile phones. |

**(i)** Which of the above conclusions is most accurate? (1 mark)

_____

**(ii)** Justify your answer to part **(i)**. You will receive one mark for good English. (4 marks)

_____

_____

_____

_____

_____

**4.** The diagram shows a ray of light entering a glass block along the normal. Complete the diagram to show the path of the light ray as it enters, passes through and exits the block. (2 marks)

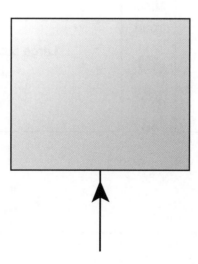

5. The diagram shows a ray of light entering a glass block. Complete the diagram to show the path of the light ray as it enters, passes through and exits the block. Make sure that the 'normal' is added to the diagram where the ray enters and exits the block. (4 marks)

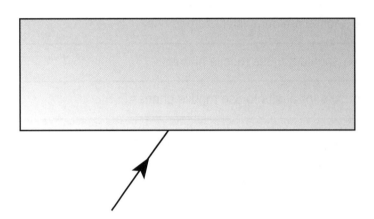

6. At some blind road junctions, a mirror is placed to allow the drivers on the minor road to see if cars are approaching from the right.

On the diagram below, draw the likely position for the mirror and draw the rays of light reflecting from it. (4 marks)

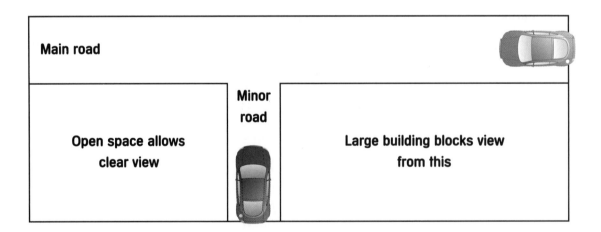

**7.** **(a)** In the space below, draw a labelled ray diagram to show how an image is formed from a plane mirror. (4 marks)

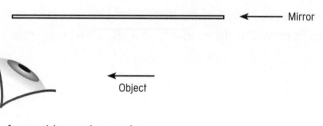

Mirror

Object

**(b)** Describe the image formed by a plane mirror. (2 marks)

......................................................................................................................................................

......................................................................................................................................................

**8.** Electromagnetic waves have a number of uses. Draw lines to match the types of waves in list A to their uses in list B. (4 marks)

**List A**

| Radio waves |

| Microwaves |

| Infrared |

| Visible light |

**List B**

| Remote controls |

| Photography |

| Satellite television |

| Television broadcasts |

**9.** **(a)** An FM radio station broadcasts at a frequency of 100MHz with a wave speed of 300 000 000m/s. Calculate the wavelength of the radio waves.

(3 marks)

**(b)** FM radio waves need a line of sight to the transmitter. Use your answer to part **(a)** and diffraction to explain why FM radio cannot be detected behind a hill, while some other radio waves can. (3 marks)

**10.** The diagram shows a wave.

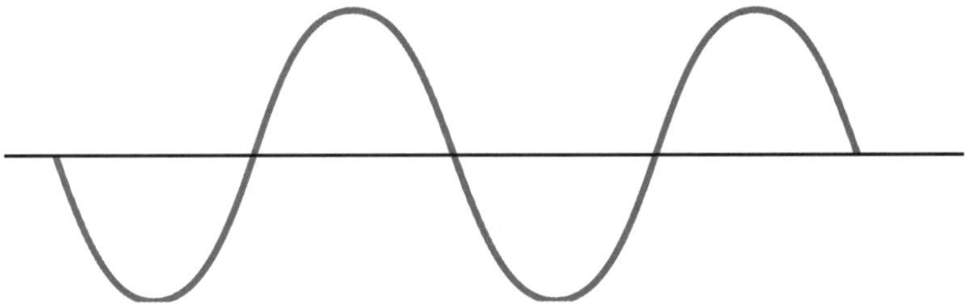

**(a)** Add labels to show the wavelength and amplitude. (2 marks)

**(b)** How many complete waves are visible on the diagram? (1 mark)

**(c)** How many complete waves would be visible if a wave travelling at the same speed but with twice the frequency was drawn? (1 mark)

**(d)** The wave shown in the diagram has a frequency of 20Hz and a wavelength of 40cm. What is the speed of the wave? (3 marks)

**11.** A wave machine at a swimming pool generates waves with a frequency of 0.5Hz.

**(a)** What does a frequency of 0.5Hz mean?   (1 mark)

........................................................................................................................................................

**(b)** The swimming pool is 50 metres long. When the machine is switched on, it takes the wave 10 seconds to travel from one end of the pool to the other. Calculate the speed of the wave.   (2 marks)

........................................................................................................................................................

........................................................................................................................................................

**(c)** Use the wave equation and your answer to part **(b)** to find the wavelength of the waves.   (4 marks)

........................................................................................................................................................

........................................................................................................................................................

........................................................................................................................................................

........................................................................................................................................................

**(d)** How many complete waves will be visible on the pool at any time?   (1 mark)

........................................................................................................................................................

**(e)** A child watching the wave machine notices that the waves change direction as they enter shallow water. What is the name for this effect?   (1 mark)

........................................................................................................................................................

**(f)** The child also notices that as the waves pass through a small opening into another pool they spread out as shown in the diagram.

(1 mark)

What name is given to this effect?

........................................................................................................................................................

**12.** An oscilloscope is used by a sound technician to measure the loudness and frequency of sounds.

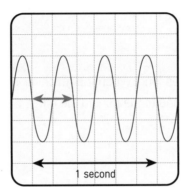

1 second

**(a)** What is sound caused by? (1 mark)

_____

**(b)** What kind of wave is a sound wave? (1 mark)

_____

**(c)** The technician looks at the trace above. The long arrow represents one second.
What is the frequency measured by the oscilloscope? (1 mark)

_____

**(d)** How would the trace appear if the same pitch sound was measured, but it was louder? (2 marks)

_____

_____

**(e)** How would the trace appear if the same loudness sound was measured, but it was higher pitched? (2 marks)

_____

_____

**(f)** The Mosquito is a device used to deter youths from hanging around in front of shops. It produces a high frequency sound that adults are not able to hear. The sound is safe but annoying.
Some people oppose the use of these devices. Suggest a reason why. (1 mark)

_____

_____

**(g)** The sound of the Mosquito reflects off nearby buildings and can be heard around corners.
What name is given to the reflection of sound? (1 mark)

_____

**13.** A spectator at a Formula 1 motor race notices that the pitch of the engine appears to change from high to low as the cars go past.

**(a)** What is the name of this effect? (1 mark)

..................................................................................................................................................

**(b)** *In this question you will be assessed on using good English, organising information clearly and using scientific terms where appropriate.*

Explain as fully as you can why the sound of a car moving away quickly will sound lower pitched. (6 marks)

..................................................................................................................................................

..................................................................................................................................................

..................................................................................................................................................

..................................................................................................................................................

..................................................................................................................................................

..................................................................................................................................................

..................................................................................................................................................

..................................................................................................................................................

**(c)** The same effect is also seen with light. What is the name of the phenomenon that occurs when the light from a distant galaxy moving away from us appears to have a longer wavelength? (1 mark)

..................................................................................................................................................

**(d)** The Andromeda galaxy is moving towards us. How will light from the Andromeda galaxy differ from most other galaxies? (1 mark)

..................................................................................................................................................

**(e)** During the 1920s, Edwin Hubble discovered that almost all galaxies appear to be moving away from one another. What conclusion about the Universe can be drawn from this? (1 mark)

..................................................................................................................................................

**14.** In the 1920s, Edwin Hubble studied the red-shift from a large number of distant galaxies and used this to calculate the speed at which they were moving away from us (recessional velocity). The graph below represents some of his findings.

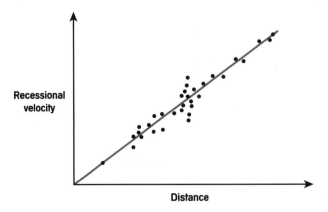

**(a)** What conclusion can be drawn from the graph? (1 mark)

_____

**(b)** Few of the points on the graph fall exactly on the line of best fit. Why might it have been difficult to get accurate measurements? (1 mark)

_____

_____

**(c)** Outline the Big Bang Theory. (2 marks)

_____

_____

_____

_____

**(d)** Hubble's finding provided some evidence in support of the Big Bang Theory. What other evidence is there to support the Big Bang Theory? (1 mark)

_____

**(e)** Not all people agree with the Big Bang Theory. Suggest why not. (2 marks)

_____

_____

_____

_____

**15.** This question is about the electromagnetic spectrum.

**(a)** Are the following statements **true** or **false**?

**(i)** Black surfaces are good reflectors of infrared radiation. (1 mark)

.................................................................................................................................

**(ii)** Gamma rays, X-rays and UV rays all have a shorter wavelength compared to visible light. (1 mark)

.................................................................................................................................

**(iii)** Radio waves, microwaves and infrared rays all have a higher frequency compared to visible light. (1 mark)

.................................................................................................................................

**(iv)** When electromagnetic waves travel through a vacuum, waves with a higher frequency travel faster than those with a lower frequency. (1 mark)

.................................................................................................................................

**(b)** Ultraviolet radiation can cause damage to the skin and lead to skin cancer. Explain how this occurs. (2 marks)

.................................................................................................................................

.................................................................................................................................

.................................................................................................................................

**(c)** The information below shows the results of a survey about the methods people use to protect themselves from UV radiation.

| Protection method | Men (%) | Women (%) |
|---|---|---|
| Hat | 40 | 30 |
| Sunscreen | 25 | 60 |

**(i)** Which method of protection is used by more women than men? (1 mark)

.................................................................................................................................

**(ii)** What ultimately would give the best protection from harmful UV rays? (1 mark)

.................................................................................................................................

**(iii)** If you apply factor 10 sunscreen, you can stay in the sun ten times as long as if you don't use sunscreen. If, on a particular day, the burn time is 20 minutes, how long could you stay in the sun before burning? (1 mark)

16. **(a)** What type of electromagnetic radiation is used by mobile phones? (1 mark)

**(b)** What are the risks generally associated with this type of radiation? (2 marks)

**(Total: ............... / 102 marks)**

# Chemistry Data Sheet

**1. Reactivity Series of Metals**

| | |
|---|---|
| Potassium | most reactive |
| Sodium | |
| Calcium | |
| Magnesium | |
| Aluminium | |
| *Carbon* | |
| Zinc | |
| Iron | |
| Tin | |
| Lead | |
| *Hydrogen* | |
| Copper | |
| Silver | |
| Gold | |
| Platinum | least reactive |

(elements in italics, though non-metals, have been included for comparison)

**2. Formulae of Some Common Ions**

**Positive ions**

| Name | Formula |
|---|---|
| Hydrogen | $H^+$ |
| Sodium | $Na^+$ |
| Silver | $Ag^+$ |
| Potassium | $K^+$ |
| Lithium | $Li^+$ |
| Ammonium | $NH_4^+$ |
| Barium | $Ba^{2+}$ |
| Calcium | $Ca^{2+}$ |
| Copper (II) | $Cu^{2+}$ |
| Magnesium | $Mg^{2+}$ |
| Zinc | $Zn^{2+}$ |
| Lead | $Pb^{2+}$ |
| Iron (II) | $Fe^{2+}$ |
| Iron (III) | $Fe^{3+}$ |
| Aluminium | $Al^{3+}$ |

**Negative ions**

| Name | Formula |
|---|---|
| Chloride | $Cl^-$ |
| Bromide | $Br^-$ |
| Fluoride | $F^-$ |
| Iodide | $I^-$ |
| Hydroxide | $OH^-$ |
| Nitrate | $NO_3^-$ |
| Oxide | $O^{2-}$ |
| Sulfide | $S^{2-}$ |
| Sulfate | $SO_4^{2-}$ |
| Carbonate | $CO_3^{2-}$ |

# Physics Equation Sheet

| | |
|---|---|
| $E = m \times c \times \theta$ | $E$ energy transferred<br>$m$ mass<br>$\theta$ temperature change<br>$c$ specific heat capacity |
| $\text{efficiency} = \dfrac{\text{useful energy out}}{\text{total energy in}} \times 100\%$ | |
| $\text{efficiency} = \dfrac{\text{useful power out}}{\text{total power in}} \times 100\%$ | |
| $E = P \times t$ | $E$ energy transferred<br>$P$ power<br>$t$ time |
| $v = f \times \lambda$ | $v$ speed<br>$f$ frequency<br>$\lambda$ wavelength |
| $s = v \times t$ | $s$ distance<br>$v$ speed<br>$t$ time |

# Periodic Table

**Key**

| relative atomic mass |
| **atomic symbol** |
| name |
| atomic (proton) number |

| 1 | 2 | | | | | | | | | | | | 3 | 4 | 5 | 6 | 7 | 0 |
|---|---|---|---|---|---|---|---|---|---|---|---|---|---|---|---|---|---|---|
| | | | | | | | | | | | | | | | | | | 4 **He** helium 2 |
| 7 **Li** lithium 3 | 9 **Be** beryllium 4 | | | | | | | | | | | | 11 **B** boron 5 | 12 **C** carbon 6 | 14 **N** nitrogen 7 | 16 **O** oxygen 8 | 19 **F** fluorine 9 | 20 **Ne** neon 10 |
| 23 **Na** sodium 11 | 24 **Mg** magnesium 12 | | | | | | | | | | | | 27 **Al** aluminium 13 | 28 **Si** silicon 14 | 31 **P** phosphorus 15 | 32 **S** sulfur 16 | 35.5 **Cl** chlorine 17 | 40 **Ar** argon 18 |
| 39 **K** potassium 19 | 40 **Ca** calcium 20 | 45 **Sc** scandium 21 | 48 **Ti** titanium 22 | 51 **V** vanadium 23 | 52 **Cr** chromium 24 | 55 **Mn** manganese 25 | 56 **Fe** iron 26 | 59 **Co** cobalt 27 | 59 **Ni** nickel 28 | 63.5 **Cu** copper 29 | 65 **Zn** zinc 30 | | 70 **Ga** gallium 31 | 73 **Ge** germanium 32 | 75 **As** arsenic 33 | 79 **Se** selenium 34 | 80 **Br** bromine 35 | 84 **Kr** krypton 36 |
| 85 **Rb** rubidium 37 | 88 **Sr** strontium 38 | 89 **Y** yttrium 39 | 91 **Zr** zirconium 40 | 93 **Nb** niobium 41 | 96 **Mo** molybdenum 42 | [98] **Tc** technetium 43 | 101 **Ru** ruthenium 44 | 103 **Rh** rhodium 45 | 106 **Pd** palladium 46 | 108 **Ag** silver 47 | 112 **Cd** cadmium 48 | | 115 **In** indium 49 | 119 **Sn** tin 50 | 122 **Sb** antimony 51 | 128 **Te** tellurium 52 | 127 **I** iodine 53 | 131 **Xe** xenon 54 |
| 133 **Cs** caesium 55 | 137 **Ba** barium 56 | 139 **La\*** lanthanum 57 | 178 **Hf** hafnium 72 | 181 **Ta** tantalum 73 | 184 **W** tungsten 74 | 186 **Re** rhenium 75 | 190 **Os** osmium 76 | 192 **Ir** iridium 77 | 195 **Pt** platinum 78 | 197 **Au** gold 79 | 201 **Hg** mercury 80 | | 204 **Tl** thallium 81 | 207 **Pb** lead 82 | 209 **Bi** bismuth 83 | [209] **Po** polonium 84 | [210] **At** astatine 85 | [222] **Rn** radon 86 |
| [223] **Fr** francium 87 | [226] **Ra** radium 88 | [227] **Ac\*** actinium 89 | [261] **Rf** rutherfordium 104 | [262] **Db** dubnium 105 | [266] **Sg** seaborgium 106 | [264] **Bh** bohrium 107 | [277] **Hs** hassium 108 | [268] **Mt** meitnerium 109 | [271] **Ds** darmstadtium 110 | [272] **Rg** roentgenium 111 | | | | | | | | |

1 **H** hydrogen 1

Elements with atomic numbers 112–116 have been reported but not fully authenticated

\*The lanthanoids (atomic numbers 58–71) and the actinoids (atomic numbers 90–103) have been omitted.

The relative atomic masses of copper and chlorine have not been rounded to the nearest whole number.